THE WILL OF GOD

IS

THE WORD OF GOD

THE WILL OF GOD

IS

THE WORD OF GOD

JAMES MACDONALD

PUBLISHING GROUP

NASHVILLE, TENNESSEE

I've been blessed to have many partners by my side in serving the Lord through more than three decades of local church ministry. Only one partner has been by my side every single day of doing God's will, and that is my wonderful, godly wife, *Kathy MacDonald,* to whom I dedicate this book.

CONTENTS

FOREWORD

I WAS STUMPED. The hard decision of buying the new house was done. The final decision was to simply choose one of four options for the color of the trim. The salesman waited patiently as I tried to visualize which color would be most aesthetically pleasing while adding to the resale value of the house. As I pondered, my friend Ron whispered to the sales rep, "You won't believe this, but *he wrote a book on decision-making.*"

Well, it's true and Ron's comment was both factual and funny because the book is *Decision Making and the Will of God.* A so-called "decision-making expert" should not struggle to pick a trim color.

However, the accusation is a bit unfair in that *Decision Making* is more than 450 pages long and more theoretical than practical. When I wrote it, I was challenging an almost universal consensus on the nature of divine guidance, so I chose to be thorough. I felt like I needed to exegete every passage, address every issue, answer every objection, and apply the principles to every significant area of life. The result was a manuscript that was both exhaustive to write and exhausting to read.

My original publisher wanted a second book closer to 150 pages in length—like *this* book. Their team was worried that a text with 24 chapters would scare potential readers away. But *Decision Making* struck a responsive chord and sold more copies than any of us had expected. So even though a shorter, more manageable version was still needed, the publisher was not interested in competing with the longer book that was selling well, and the second book never got off the drawing board.

Thankfully, Pastor James MacDonald recognized the same need and did something about it. He studied the Scriptures and came to the same conclusions articulated in *Decision Making.* Then he wrote his own book: *The Will of God IS the Word of God.* It is much more than a pared-down version of someone else's ideas. MacDonald has given the church a rich exposition of biblical truth filled with wise insight and challenging motivation.

Yes, this book is shorter, but it is also a pleasure to read. I used to teach a preaching class at Multnomah University. My favorite lecture was called, "Paint a picture with your words." At the end of the class, I gave a week-long assignment to look for pictures in life that could bring color and clarity to a sermon. I then handed the students small paintbrushes that they were required to carry with them all week. MacDonald was not in my class, but he writes with a paintbrush in each hand.

James MacDonald communicates with the passion of an articulate preacher and the gentle touch of a caring pastor. He has a gift for expressing practical theology in ways that instruct and inspire the reader to put principles into practice. This book is especially useful for the reader who is saying, "I need help for this decision *right now*." His nine questions to ask before making any decision are filled with biblical wisdom. They give readers guidance and confidence that it is possible to make decisions that are godly and wise.

For some readers, this book will represent a paradigm shift. Haddon Robinson said that "Sacred cows make the best hamburger, but the meat can be hard to swallow." MacDonald helps readers digest new ideas by skillfully marinating the "truth in love." I believe your initial taste test will whet your appetite for successive courses of a delicious meal.

Don't tell my publisher I said this, but if you can only buy one book on decision-making according to the will of God, this would be a great choice.

Garry Friesen, PhD
Professor of Bible
Africa College of Theology
Kigali, Rwanda

AN INVITATION

IS THERE ANY human experience that exceeds the joy of knowing for certain that we are smack-dab in the center of God's will? When we know with confidence that we're doing the will of God, then we know that all is well, no matter what is wrong in our lives. And when we don't feel confident that we're doing the will of God, then it almost doesn't matter what else is going well in life. This insidious, unsettled uncertainty eats at us. "Am I really doing God's will?" We wonder. We worry.

Compounding that sense of insecurity is a lot of unbiblical teaching on the subject of God's will, which muddies the waters even more. **"Therefore do not be foolish, but understand what the will of the Lord *IS*"** (Eph. 5:17, emphasis mine). There are a lot of things that God's will isn't, but there's only one thing that it *IS*.

Unlike what most of us have been taught, God's will is not about where we are or even necessarily whom we are with, but about *who* we are. **"For this *IS* the will of God,"** Paul writes, **"your sanctification"** (1 Thess. 4:3, emphasis mine). When we are increasingly the people God wants us to be, then we can be confident we are where God wants us to be and with whom God wants us to be.

In other words, your character traits, spiritual priorities, and manner of living—what Christians have for twenty centuries called "holiness"—this is the will of God. And when your life increasingly conforms to God's prescription for holiness, then all of these nonsensical sidetracks of geography or which couch to buy or where to go to dinner tonight fade to the shadows, and you can live in the glorious freedom of what the will of God *IS* instead of searching out a nonexistent who and where, etc. Stated simply, the will of God *IS* about who you are. The will of God *IS* about your sanctification, that refining process in which you are conformed more and more into the image of Christ Jesus.

So you don't need a road map for life, spelling out every twist and turn, every choice you need to make. There is no specific blueprint, and God's knowledge of the future means you don't have to figure it out in advance of joyfully experiencing it under His watchful care.

All you really need is a book detailing the kind of person God wants you to be, and you have that Book. The will of

God *IS* the Word of God. The Word of God *IS* the will of God. Each *IS* true. And that discovery leads to a glorious experience of freedom for every Christ-follower. You no longer need to worry and wonder about the minute details of life. If you are increasingly the person God wants you to be, then you can be confident you are living the fullest and most joyful life possible. That, in the end, encapsulates for you personally what the will of God actually *IS*.

We haven't arrived yet. We are works in progress. When we look around this beautiful, created world—from towering mountain peaks to the silver moon at night to the sun falling on our windows in the morning, signaling a new day with fresh mercies—no matter where we look, we see God's creative genius on display. Everything that God made, He made instantly, completely, and perfectly. But in His will, He did not make His children immediately and perfectly. No, He's making us gradually and consistently, refining us over time. We know that inherent in God's creative act is the desire to perfect what He has made—including us. The will of God is to perfect the pinnacle of His creation, His children who have been reconciled to Him through faith in Christ. This is what God is doing in the world today. He's changing His kids, little by little. **"But we all, with unveiled face, beholding as in a mirror the glory of the Lord, are being transformed into the same image from glory to glory, just as from the Lord, the Spirit"** (2 Cor. 3:18 NASB). How awesome to know that the will of God begins and ends with **"this *IS* the will of God, your sanctification"** (1 Thess. 4:3, emphasis mine).

Are these assertions about God's will hard to accept? Do they stretch your current theology or challenge your previous understanding? Have no fear because we can trust God to show us His will about His will from His Word.

I invite you on a journey with me to explore what God's will *IS* by studying what the Bible actually says about that elusive phrase, "the will of God." Together let's determine to be free, once and for all, from the burdensome quest to discover what it isn't or feel guilty about something God never intended at all. Then, through this biblical certainty, we can revel and rest from now till forever in what the will of the Lord actually *IS*.

CHAPTER 1

Who Needs God's Will?

DO YOU WONDER about God's will for your life personally? Do you ponder specific decisions you need to make and if they are in line with God's will? It might reassure you to know that most believers frequently wrestle with God's will for their lives. Welcome to the puzzle party!

But wait. Should exploring the topic of God's will be a party? Or do we have to relegate it to a serious, dusty, library crusade? Fear not, whenever we're with Jesus, we need not lose the idea of celebration. Jesus was constantly attending parties with His friends. In fact, He was accused of too much frivolity (Mark 2:16). Understanding God's will is not the absence of celebration; it is, in fact, a much better way to get there. The joy of knowing what God's will actually *IS* and doing it far exceeds the shallow pleasantries of what we typically mean by "party time."

So where do we begin? **"Therefore do not be foolish, but understand what the will of the Lord *IS*"** (Eph. 5:17, emphasis mine). How well do we actually understand God's will? Take the following quiz to find out how clear or fuzzy God's will seems to you. Mark each statement TRUE or FALSE.

_____   1. God has a specific plan for my life that I should discover and follow.

_____   2. The little intuitions or promptings I feel are God's way of revealing His will to me. When I feel a tiny twinge or a holy hunch, that's God talking to me, guiding me into His will.

_____   3. Feeling a sense of peace is a key factor in making godly decisions.

_____   4. It is wise to use a "fleece" in determining God's will. (If you are unfamiliar with the term "fleece," then skip this question. We will address it later.)

_____   5. God's will can be divided into two categories: God's perfect will and God's permissive will.

_____   6. When faced with two good options, I must be careful not to make the wrong decision.

_____   7. Some people are called to full-time ministry; others are called to non-vocational, "lay" ministry.

The Answer Key

Let's quickly review the answers to the true/false statements from the quiz. In later chapters, we will address these issues in greater depth, and the answers will become clearer as we examine what God's Word teaches about His will. For now, a biblical answer and brief comments.

1. **God has a specific plan for my life that I should discover and follow.**

   And the Bible says . . . False.

   God does not have a one-track route for your life devoid of meaningful choices that you must figure out. While some popular verses are used to support the "specific, detailed plan" approach to God's will, when we study those passages more closely, we will see that they don't support that conclusion.

2. **The little intuitions or promptings I feel are God's way of revealing His will to me. When I feel a tiny twinge or a holy hunch, that's God talking to me, guiding me into His will.**

   And the Bible says . . . False.

   How can we tell if that pit-in-our-stomachs feeling is a holy hunch or last night's pizza? Our feelings can be so misleading. The advice to "just follow your heart" is not just bad counsel; it's also dangerous! Your heart (and mine) **"is deceitful above all things, and desperately sick; who can understand it?"** (Jer. 17:9). Our hearts are terrible leaders, so filled with variance and vacillation.

And here's a little heads-up: Doesn't it seem as though people who rely on hunches and promptings to discern God's will end up doing what they wanted to do all along?

3. Feeling a sense of peace is a key factor in making godly decisions.

And the Bible says . . . False. (This is beginning to seem like a pattern, isn't it?)

I am amazed at how often I hear people claim to be completely "at peace" about directly disobeying what God clearly says in His Word! Christians say these things so often we cease to even question their legitimacy. It reminds me of the guy who said, "When I die I want to go peacefully in my sleep like Grandpa, not screaming and alert like the people in the car he was driving." Get it? Peaceful isn't always good and isn't always God's will.

4. It is wise to use a "fleece" in determining God's will.

And the Bible says . . . False.

Although "fleece" rhymes with "peace," that's not why this statement is also false. It is false because God never prescribes fleeces as a way to determine His guidance. If you are curious about the origin of this notion of fleeces, read the story of Gideon in Judges 6–8. While Gideon's fleece is interesting and memorable, we have to remember as we read his story that Gideon already knew God's will before he set out a fleece! He had heard God's will from the mouth of the angel of the Lord. The fleece was an overly needy confirmation that God graciously granted, but Gideon was failing to live by faith in what God had said. Remember that story portions of Scripture record what actually happened, which is not always instructive on what should happen. Too often making precepts out of narrative gets us confused about what God's will actually *IS*.

5. **God's will can be divided into two categories: God's perfect will and God's permissive will.**

   And the Bible says . . . False.

   You may have heard those terms before, and they sound so meaningful and theological that you may have accepted them as correct. But our standard of measurement is biblical, and those terms aren't supported by the Bible. Often those who use these terms are motivated to protect God's reputation, but God can protect His own reputation. We have to avoid being foolish and instead chase hard after what the Bible actually says about God's will.

6. **When faced with two good options, I must be careful not to make the wrong decision.**

  And the Bible says . . . False.

  This concept alone can be crippling for Christians who want to please God. The thought process goes like this: *I see two good choices, but only one of those can be God's will. If I choose the wrong option, I end up in a scary place outside God's will.*

  Although this sounds like sober thinking and gives our choices significant weight, the Bible does not teach this. Every day you face multiple, good alternatives from which to choose. If every step, every turn, every door you open has to be the single one that matches God's will, then life will quickly feel like a nightmare. The Christian life will feel like a field full of land mines. As we will see clearly and refreshingly, God's Word actually teaches that God's will has a ton of freedom within it.

> God's Word gives us a ton of freedom within God's will.

7. **Some people are called to full-time ministry; others are called to non-vocational, "lay" ministry.**

  And the Bible says . . . False.

  How does this fit into our exploration of God's will? Some people use this line of thinking to justify a wrong approach to God's will. They reason that certain "professional" Christians need to worry about following God's will, while the rest of us can take it easy discerning God's will because we are only doing ministry "on the side." Fortunately, our job description is more straightforward than that. We are all simply Christians, servants and followers of Jesus Christ— and the Bible nowhere distinguishes between professional and amateur Christians.

Audience Responses

When I present these statements to people, I can almost feel the heated objections rising from the crowd. Some of these viewpoints are long-held, cherished guidelines in people's approach to life. When I call these ideas false, they struggle not to fold their arms, signaling their resistance. It can be very unsettling to rethink some of our deep, foundational concepts about God, what it looks like to follow Him, and what His will actually *IS*.

But at this point, we need to gently remind ourselves that we must base our principles on what God says—not on what other people say about and for Him. I readily include myself in that "other people" category and challenge you to check everything I write against your Bible. As always, compare what you hear and believe against God's never-changing Word.

Motivation

As we begin to untie the knots in our view of God's will, let's consider three reasons we should explore the topic of God's will (besides just our own burning curiosity on what God's will actually *IS*).

Motivation #1: Because there's so much **misunderstanding** on the subject. As our quiz likely revealed, even many well-meaning, thoughtful Christians who have been walking with God for years have some distorted ideas about God's will.

Motivation #2: Because there's widespread **abuse** of this subject. Many of us have discovered the almost magical power of using the phrase, "It's God's will," when we are talking about our plans or desires for the future. Too many Christians drop the phrase in a conversation like a trump card, overruling all other opinions and viewpoints. After all, who can argue when someone asserts, "It's God's will"?

When someone claims, "This is God's will for me," it is a definite verbal straight-arm! Another variation of that claim is, "This is what God told me to do." Are we allowed to ask any more questions when someone drops the "God told me" grenade in front of all objection to their new life trajectory? Were we not just told to back off? Nobody wants to be accused of trying to contradict God, if in fact He has spoken—but has He? It can't be God's will for me to block someone else from doing God's will.

But does announcing our new plans as God's will make them unaccountable to others we are supposed to be living in community with? Is it possible that we have, in some cases, used the phrase "God's will" to make getting our way easier?

When I hear claims like these, I don't feel reassured that God's will is faithfully being done; I feel uncomfortable. How can anyone offer caution or counsel to someone declaring divine direction without equivocation? My discomfort grows even worse when people look me in the eye and tell me, "God told me to tell you to _____." Interestingly, this message often relates to what our church is doing wrong, and the warning they are delivering for God is the exact same as their known assessment of our ministry. God handily confirmed their personal evaluation in the exact same words they use? With backup like that, who can argue? I have learned not to engage this line of argument, as people playing this trump card are not really interested in mutually enlightening dialogue.

> How can anyone offer caution or counsel to someone declaring divine direction without equivocation?

Especially important is avoiding anyone who proclaims a directive from God about His will that blatantly contradicts Scripture. My prayer is that some carefully studied teaching from Scripture can help us all avoid these kind of abuses, choosing instead to live in the glorious liberty of what God's will actually *IS*.

Motivation #3: Because there's widespread **consternation** about this subject. As a pastor, I hear frequent frustration from God's people about the elusive subject of God's will and the false guilt people feel for not confidently finding what God's will *IS*. While those feelings of frustration aren't fun, they are a hopeful sign. People who are fed up with confusion are hungry for the truth.

Most Christians I know are deeply desirous of God's direction—if only they could grasp what His will *IS*. Tying to Ephesians 5:17, they feel foolish because they don't yet **"understand what the will of the Lord is,"** but they *want* to understand! They are frustrated with a view of God's will that sounds holy but is wholly elusive and unlivable.

Jesus said, **"My food is to do the will of him who sent me and to accomplish his work"** (John 4:34). Is that your desire? Do you want to know and live according to God's will?

Then welcome to our traveling band on the journey to discover what God's will *IS*.

Heavenly Father,

For those who feel confused about Your will, I ask You for clarity.

For those who feel abused by human teaching about Your will, I ask You for healing.

For those who have abused the topic of Your will by using it as leverage, I ask You for honest self-evaluation.

And for those who are flat-out frustrated and determined to understand Your will so they can obey it, I ask You for light, truth, and power.

Fill all of us with a growing desire to know and love You and to live out Your will.

In the name of Jesus, who came to give us abundant life. Amen.

CHAPTER 2

God's Will from God's Word

DOES GOD HAVE a will for each individual? Has God actually designed a specific, detailed plan for every person? Does God have an unpublished paint-by-number canvas representing your life, and the only way the picture is going to look exactly right is if you discover the intended colors and paint them on the correct numbers?

This certainly sounds like something God *could* do—after all, He is God—but is that what He *would* do? Has God actually structured our lives like a mystery puzzle we have to piece together?

Consider this classic example of the God's will question: "What does God want me to do regarding further education?" That's both a personal question and a family question. It's a bank account question and a test scores question. But is it a God's will question?

If you spend time with believing high school seniors, you can almost feel the tension in their rapid-fire thoughts. *Where does God want me to go to college? I can't figure it out. I've visited a dozen campuses, and I can't decide where I'm supposed to go. Does God have a will for me? Has God chosen the specific college I should attend? Will He tell me? If not, how does He expect me to figure it out? How many colleges are there in this country anyway? What if I pick the wrong one? What happens if I make a bad choice?* This string of all-too-common questions haunts students who want to follow God but don't know how.

And that's just the start. A few years later, a new set of questions crops up. *Who should I marry? Who should I spend the rest of my life with? What if I'm here, but that person is somewhere far away? Or what if we are passing each other every day but just haven't been introduced? I want to marry the person God chose for me. My parents have been praying for that person ever since I was a little kid. Somewhere out there is the person I should marry, and it's like finding a needle in a haystack. How many people are in this country anyway? But what if my person is in Bolivia? How will we meet? Do I have to wait for God to work it out magically, or is there something I'm supposed to be doing?*

Maybe you've moved beyond these issues to home, career, and health choices. Or perhaps looking back at your decisions, you feel waves of regret as you wonder if you missed God's will. Did you make a quick pick (or several), and now you live with the awful sense that you are on a different path than the one God intended for you? Is it like you took a permanent detour, and you can't seem to find a route back to the narrow way of God's will?

If we're honest with ourselves, many of us have wrestled with these questions. We have worried and wallowed at times in this confusion. The burning question lingers in the back of our minds: What is God's will for my life?

So now I have to ask you a question: Do you really want to know the answer?

Knowing God and what He wants for your life isn't a casual endeavor. It's not for the weak person who loses interest after five minutes, distracted by the next thought that flies past. The answer isn't packaged in 140 tweet characters or in a catchy slogan to sing in the shower. It's laid out in depth, in detail, in God's Book—but you have to spend time digging it out.

Let me tell you that God does, in fact, have a will for your life. If you want to know it—if you really, really want to know what God wants for you—then read on.

But first, before we consider specifics, let's step back for a big picture perspective.

What Is a Will?

Rocks don't have wills. Trees don't have wills. Humans have wills. A *will* encompasses a person's awareness, desire, planning, decisions, and actions. Another word for will is *volition*, which is the capacity to weigh options and discriminate based upon assessed value. It's the ability to choose based upon perception of advantage or disadvantage.

We have wills. Because we are made in God's image, our wills are an imperfect reflection of His. As the Creator, God has the supreme will; as creatures, we have limited wills. God wills the advantage of others in Himself. We too can choose beyond immediate gratification or the pure self-advantage of animals.

> A *will* encompasses a person's awareness, desire, planning, decisions, and actions.

A defining characteristic the Scriptures reveal about God is that He has a will and gave you a will to exercise. Is understanding His will something revealed in Scripture or merely a human construct?

Welcome to Theology Class

If you ever audit a theology class on spiritual formation, you may hear the concept of God's will broken into three categories. The terminology varies, but the classic terms used to describe God's will are the following:

1. God's sovereign will
2. God's moral will
3. God's individual will (more on this in chapter 3)

Does this pattern reflect how God actually relates to people? Is this paradigm valid? As I mentioned before (and will keep hammering over and over again), any time we hear teaching about God, our first task is to check it against Scripture. If these three categories of God's will are sound, then we should find biblical evidence that teaches and illustrates them. All in favor of some detective work?

God's Sovereign Will

Hundreds of years before the birth of Jesus Christ, God gave the prophet Isaiah a vivid description: **"A voice cries: 'In the wilderness prepare the way of the LORD; make straight in the desert a highway for our God. Every valley shall be lifted up, and every mountain and hill be made low; the uneven ground shall become level, and the rough places a plain. And the glory of the LORD shall be revealed, and all flesh shall see it together, for the mouth of the LORD has spoken'"** (Isa. 40:3–5).

You may recognize the opening of Isaiah 40:3 as a prophetic description of John the Baptist, who would come on the scene centuries later and prepare the way for the Messiah. John's was the voice crying out and confronting the people of his day to get ready for the Lord.

Isaiah 40:4–5 describes how nothing hinders God's progress. Nothing gets in His way. He fills valleys. He flattens hills. No obstacle prevents His plan. What God says He will do, He does. If God speaks, consider it a done deal. This is a clear description of God's sovereign will—God's declaration of what He will do.

The word *sovereign* means supreme in power and without equal. The role of a sovereign, or king, is superior in position to all others. God's sovereign will is the combination of God's secret purposes, plan, and power that controls the outcome of all matters in the universe. Only God's will is sovereign because God alone has the means to carry out whatever He wills.

> Nothing thwarts God's sovereign will. Whatever God says will happen, does happen—on time, every time.

Stop and make an indelible note of this in your thinking. Nothing thwarts God's sovereign will. Whatever God says will happen, does happen—on time, every time. God never paces back and forth in heaven, wringing His hands. He's not wondering how things will turn out. He knows because He decreed it before the foundation of the world. He doesn't stand on tiptoe, peering at us to see what will happen next. Our sovereign God rules the universe with His feet up.

The conflicts and seeming chaos in our world do not stress God or stretch Him in any way. He is in complete and total control. Let's look together at eight Bible passages that showcase God's sovereign will. We will see how God's will is a secret plan that controls the outcome of all matters in the universe, from wars to elections to weather patterns. Everything and everyone is in the mix—sickness, sin, kings, presidents, and paupers alike. From criminals to home school moms, from evil to good, every member of the human race, regardless of philosophy or theology, is a fully cooperating participant in God's sovereign will, because nobody can thwart Him. Nothing does. The world is going where God wants it to go. History is headed in His direction. God is at the wheel, and understanding God's sovereignty is foundational to fully knowing and appreciating what God's will *IS*. Consider the following eight passages as a way of "coloring in" this beautiful concept of God's sovereign will.

#1: Sovereign over Human Power

"The king's heart is a stream of water in the hand of the LORD; he turns it wherever he will" (Prov. 21:1).

To the original readers of this proverb, the highest human sovereign was the king. Kings had unchecked, absolute authority over their kingdoms. There was no balance of power or three branches of government to keep a ruler in check. Yet this proverb asserts that the king is in God's hands, so any human ruler or authority is under God's control.

What was true of God then is still true today. Whether we are thinking about the heart of our current president or any other leader on the face of the earth, God **"turns it wherever he will."** If the rulers make good decisions, God uses them. If the rulers make bad decisions, God uses them. God is in complete and total control, ensuring that every human action is channeled like a river toward the ocean of His sovereign plan.

#2: Sovereign over Human Objections

The book of Daniel is the next stop on our tour of God's sovereignty. **"All the inhabitants of the earth are accounted as nothing, and he does according to his will among the host of heaven and among the inhabitants of the earth; and none can stay his hand or say to him, 'What have you done?'"** (Dan. 4:35).

God does what He wants, whenever He wants. We cannot stop Him, nor does the Lord respond when we object to His sovereign will. **"What have you done?"** is an accountability question asked by one in authority over another. We ask this question of our children or our employees. We don't ask this question of God and expect an answer. The point here isn't that we can't ask God hard questions; the point is that we can't demand answers from God. He doesn't account to us or owe us anything.

The text also points out **"the inhabitants of the earth are accounted as nothing."** Does that suggest that God doesn't love us? Not at all! God does love us; we just don't influence or earn that love. We cannot direct Him or control Him. God's decisions are not subject to a vote of approval or influenced by opinion polls. We may not like some of the things God is doing, and God certainly won't hammer us for expressing our feelings. But He doesn't change His plans to please any of us. God does not need human approval before He acts. He has His reasons and His purposes for all that He does, and it all falls into the category of His sovereign will—which in the end, every mouth will agree is good. (See Mark 7:37, which says the people agreed that He does all things well.)

#3: Sovereign over the Son

"This Jesus, delivered up according to the definite plan and foreknowledge of God, you crucified and killed by the hands of lawless men" (Acts 2:23).

Was God surprised when Jesus was crucified? Did Jesus' death throw God the Father off a little bit? Did God have to go to plan B? No. Acts 2:23 calls the cross God's **"definite plan and foreknowledge."** Oh, He knew! Jesus is the **"Lamb slain from the foundation of the world"** (Rev. 13:8 NKJV).

Notice how Acts 2:23 combines God's master plan with the evil actions of sinful people. Even when these people were doing wrong, when they were killing God's Son, when they were getting rid of their "Jesus problem"—even then, God's sovereign plan was unfolding. That's how His will is carried out on earth as it is in heaven, despite and even through the wicked schemes of human beings.

#4: Sovereign over Opposition

The prayers of early Christians show us that they recognized God's sovereign will. **"For truly in this city there were gathered together against your holy servant Jesus, whom you anointed, both Herod and Pontius Pilate, along with the Gentiles and the peoples of Israel, to do whatever your hand and your plan had predestined to take place"** (Acts 4:27–28).

Here's the backdrop to the story: One day Peter and John went to the temple to pray, and a beggar, lame from birth, asked them for money. Through the two disciples, God miraculously healed this man. For the first time in his life, the man took a step, and he began **"walking and leaping and praising God"** (Acts 3:8)!

The miracle that freed the man became the false premise for Peter and John's arrest. The religious guys were bent that Jesus' followers were working miracles and proclaiming the resurrected Christ. The early church was growing and with it the pressure of persecution, prison, and death. After intense questioning and murderous threats, Peter and John were eventually released. As soon as they were free, the two disciples gathered their friends and voiced a prayer that reflected their true faith in sovereign God's will. Although powerful people were determined to silence them, just as they had tried to muzzle the Lord Jesus, the believers were confident that nothing could happen apart from **"whatever your hand and your plan had predestined to take place"** (Acts 4:28). Facing death threats, these Christians trusted in God's sovereign will. They knew that when people are doing right, God uses it, and when people are doing wrong, God uses even their evil actions to bring about His purposes. God always has His way.

#5: Sovereign over Human Will

If your mind isn't spinning yet from considering God's sovereign will, then read Paul's words to the Romans. **"So then he has mercy on whomever he wills, and he hardens whomever he wills"** (Rom. 9:18).

God gives mercy when He wants to give mercy, and God hardens the heart of a person when He wants to. It's His sovereign choice. Nothing can stop His will.

In Romans 9, Paul was describing the hardest God-hardened heart in the Bible: Pharaoh's. Each time Moses made his request, **"Let my people go"** (Exod. 5:1; 7:16; 8:1; 9:1; 10:3; etc.), Pharaoh hardened his heart—or it was hardened for him. It's a mysterious and awful sequence to watch:

"Still Pharaoh's heart was hardened" (Exod. 7:13).

"He hardened his heart" (8:15).

"But the heart of Pharaoh was hardened" (9:7).

"But the LORD hardened the heart of Pharaoh" (9:12).

"He sinned yet again and hardened his heart" (9:34).

"But the LORD hardened Pharaoh's heart" (10:20).

Did Pharaoh harden his own heart? Yes. Did God also harden Pharaoh's heart? Yes. Somehow God exerted His will in the direction of Pharaoh's own will to confirm his stubborn choices. God had reasons we don't entirely understand, but sometimes it strikes us as unfair. After all, **"who can resist his will?"** (Rom. 9:19).

Yet we need to remind ourselves that we are in no position to judge fairness, in the same way an ant is in no position to judge the horizon on Mars. Be assured that God, whose viewpoint infinitely exceeds our own, has a standard of justice to match. We tend to think of fairness as "what is best for me." God sees the big picture. He takes in the farthest horizon of space and time in all directions at once. The theme of Romans 9 is how God, by His sovereign will, made arrangements for Gentiles (including those of us who believe) to be candidates for salvation. Before we blame God for being unfair, we have to remember that we are the primary beneficiaries of His "unfairness"! God's sovereign will does what is universally best to achieve all He planned and chose to accomplish in human history.

Riding the Boat of God's Sovereignty

Let's try to wrap our minds around this seeming tension between our human wills and God's sovereign will. Imagine that we are taking a cruise to England. The ocean liner has left

New York harbor en route to Liverpool. Nobody is going to disrupt this ship's course. Yet here we are on the boat, making decisions about how to spend our time. Perhaps you choose to play ping-pong, while other people are swimming in the pool. Passengers are doing their own thing all over the boat. Each person is operating as an independent moral agent, making individual choices while moving about the ship and all enjoying its many options for activity. Yet the passengers' choices don't alter the reality that this ocean liner is going to England, and no choice of theirs is going to stop it. In that way, God has some sovereign purposes in this world. The little choices we make will never alter His purposes. Even though I choose what to do on the boat, that ship is sailing to England.

#6: Sovereign over E-v-e-r-y-t-h-i-n-g!

Maybe you wonder about things you believe are outside God's will. To answer that, let's visit the classic New Testament statement on God's sovereign will. In the introduction of his letter to the Ephesian Christians, Paul affirmed that their inclusion in God's grace was part of God's purpose. Their salvation was God's sovereign plan. **"In him we have obtained an inheritance, having been predestined according to the purpose of him who works all things according to the counsel of his will"** (Eph. 1:11).

What does God use to work His will? God uses **"all things."** Some things? Convenient things? Easy things? No,

He uses **"all things."** (See also Rom. 8:28, another beloved **"all things"** statement.) Nothing stumps God. He uses **"all things"** in His master plan, driving the course of human history toward His sovereign ends and for His glory.

#7: Sovereign Even over Little Things

"The lot is cast into the lap, but its every decision is from the LORD" (Prov. 16:33).

In biblical times, casting lots was a decision-making method. It was like drawing straws, flipping a coin, or rolling dice. The lot was cast into someone's lap. A person's robe could be stretched between his legs to form a firm surface to receive the lot. Though this decision-making process seems to be based on pure chance, the proverb says that God controls the outcome of every decision. It doesn't matter what you do; it doesn't matter what I do. Although every football team flips a coin to determine who kicks off, God ultimately controls even the little things, such as how that coin lands and who gets the first chance to score.

#8: Sovereign over the Universe

"Worthy are you, our Lord and God, to receive glory and honor and power, for you created all things, and by your will they existed and were created" (Rev. 4:11).

Why is there a universe? Because God willed it.

Why is there a solar system? Because God willed it.

Why is there a planet called Earth? Because God willed it.

Why do you exist today? Why do you get to draw another breath this moment? Because God willed it. You are here by His design and purpose. And you can have a part in His purpose. Even your participation is within God's sovereign will. Everything God wants to happen, happens. Even when something happens that grieves Him, He uses it to accomplish what He does want. That's God's sovereign will.

Do things happen in this world that God doesn't want to happen? Yes! They all fit into a giant category called Sin. In fact, many or even most of the things that are happening in our world are things that God doesn't want. Is He stressed about it? No. He works like a master chess player—no matter what move we make, God makes the next move, and His purposes continue forward unhindered and without delay. That's God's sovereign will.

The Master Chess Player

Fully explaining God's sovereignty is an impossible task. No human words or analogies can do it justice. The best illustration I have been able to find came from Indonesia and a guy named Don.

More than twenty years ago, Kathy and I went on a missions trip to Indonesia, and there we met a renowned missionary named Don Richardson, who wrote *Peace Child* and *Lords of the Earth,* books filled with moving stories of God's love for lost people. We were there with our friends, Don's son Steve and daughter-in-law Arlene. When Don showed up, I learned a new piece of Don Richardson trivia: he is a chess Master.

A chess Master? I had never even heard this term. "Chess Master" is an official title given to an expert at chess. Don said, "I'm going to play twelve people at the same time." Now, I consider myself decent at chess, but I didn't even make the cut to be one of the twelve opponents. Still I was fascinated to see how this worked.

Twelve people lined up on one side of the table with twelve chessboards in front of them. While the players made their first moves, Don walked up and down the table, talking to us at the same time, and he would make a move. He never looked at one of the games for more than three or four seconds.

In less than ten minutes, Don had beaten them all.

Several of his opponents were stunned. They were strong chess players who had been champions in high school.

But this was a chess Master. They didn't stand a chance against him.

That to me is a small picture of God's sovereignty. No matter what move we make, God always knows the next move to advance His purposes and assure His victory.

If I make a good move—God makes a better one and ends up winning.

If I make a bad move—no problem, God makes an awesome move and still wins.

God is the chess Master—nothing we do, good or bad, limits His sovereignty.

God's Moral Will

If God's sovereign will encompasses His planned purposes and the power to bring them about, then God's moral will relates to the human behavior He prescribes in His Word. God's moral will is how He wants us to behave, what He tells us in the Bible to love, and what He wants us to hate. God's moral will is the God-given prescription for human behavior, inspired by the Holy Spirit (2 Tim. 3:16–17) and recorded in the Bible.

"Moral will" is not a biblical term, and I suppose that causes some confusion. Certainly God's will for human behavior involves our morality, but it is far more than that, so I prefer to call it God's "written will." My sincere request would be that every time you ever again hear the phrase "God's moral will" you would

> God's moral will is the God-given prescription for human behavior, inspired by the Holy Spirit (2 Tim. 3:16–17) and recorded in the Bible.

immediately translate that by saying to yourself, "That means God's written will, the Bible."

God's stated desires, what He wants us to choose as we make decisions moment by moment, form His "moral will." (That means God's written will, the Bible! Just testing you.) **"Behold, you delight in truth in the inward being"** (Ps. 51:6). That inner truth is our conformity in action and attitude, in what we do and don't do, in what we think/feel and don't think/feel. Everything that God wants to have happen, that we can choose to participate in, the totality of God's expectation for human behavior, is revealed in Scripture. Second Peter 1:3 states that God **"has granted to us all things that pertain to life and godliness."** That is God's written will (the Bible). God's sovereign will includes His settled, secret purposes that will surely come about. God's moral will is His written expectations for human behavior, which are completely detailed in the Bible. Beyond that, the central supposition of this book is that God does not have a specific or detailed will for the individual—just His sovereign will covering what He is going to accomplish and His written will, the Bible, covering all that we can do to participate with Him. This is why we say, "The will of God *IS* the Word of God." The Bible includes all the specifics God commands us to obey as our means to participate as individuals in accomplishing His sovereign will.

Curious readers are probably wondering at this point, "Then what is God's will for me personally?" Good question. Fortunately, the Bible applies to you the same way it applies to every other human being. God practices equal opportunity engagement when it comes to His will. His will *IS* His Word, and you have the chance to believe and obey, just like everyone else. In fact, that is what His will for you *IS*.

> This is why we say, "The will of God *IS* the Word of God." The Bible includes all the specifics God commands us to obey as our means to participate as individuals in accomplishing His sovereign will.

God's Will *Is* for You to Be Saved

The Lord offers salvation to all (see Isa. 45:21–22; 55:1; Matt. 11:28; Acts 17:30; 1 Tim. 2:3–4; Rev. 22:17). And because He is **"not wishing that any should perish"** (2 Pet. 3:9), He extends human history so more and more can be saved. At the same time, His sovereign will **"chose us in him before the foundation of the world"** (Eph. 1:4). So in His sovereignty, did God choose us? Yes. Did He also give us the opportunity to choose Him? Yes. Does your head hurt yet? This is what the apostle Paul described as **"the mystery of his will"** (Eph. 1:9). In this life, we will never be able to fully reconcile those two concepts in our minds—and that's okay.

According to Deuteronomy 29:29, **"The secret things belong to the** Lord **our God"** (His sovereign will) **"but the things that are revealed"** (His written will, the Bible) **"belong to us and to our children forever, that we may do all the words of this law"** (again, the Bible).

God has not revealed how His sovereign will and His written will fit together on the issue of salvation. But of this you can be sure: God wants you to be converted. **"The Lord is . . . not wishing that [you] should perish"** (2 Pet. 3:9). God doesn't want you to go to hell and pay the penalty for your own sin. Jesus died on the cross and gave His life as an atoning sacrifice for your sin. If you will turn from your sin and embrace Christ by faith, then God will count your sin debt as paid by Christ, forgiving you entirely and eternally. Only through Christ can you receive the gift of eternal life. Have you done that? If not, God's will is for you to receive the forgiveness of Jesus Christ by faith *right now.* **"Today, if you hear his voice, do not harden your hearts"** (Heb. 3:15). If you receive Him by faith, you become His. **"But to all who did receive him, who believed in his name, he gave the right to become children of God"** (John 1:12). It's God's will for you to be saved.

God's Will *IS* for You to Be Sanctified

In the fourth chapter of Paul's first letter to the Thessalonian Christians, he gives this wonderfully clarifying summation: **"For this is the will of God, your sanctifica-tion . . ."** (1 Thess. 4:3). The next time someone asks you, "What is God's will for me?" or even if you've been wondering yourself, search no further for your answer. God wants all of His children to be sanctified!

Once you grasp what sanctification is, you'll have plenty to keep you busy doing God's will for the rest of your life. Every morning when you wake up, you can ask, "What's God's will for me today?" And the answer is the same every morning: "My sanctification." That's an awesome, biblical answer that will more than occupy you all day.

What is sanctification? *Sanctification* is the lifelong process in which Christ-followers are refined and increas-ingly conformed to the behavior pattern of Jesus Christ. **"And we all, with unveiled face, behold-ing the glory of the Lord, are being transformed into the same image from one degree of glory to another"** (2 Cor. 3:18). Sanctification is the work of God in the lives of forgiven sinners that takes them step by step away from selfish, sinful patterns of liv-ing and more and more into a life that is wholly holy and set

> *Sanctification* is the lifelong process in which Christ-followers are refined and increasingly conformed to the behavior pattern of Jesus Christ.

apart entirely for the glory of Jesus Christ. To be sanctified is to live in complete, continuous submission to Him.

Regardless of the hospital or home birth you experienced, even if you arrived on terra firma in a cab on the way to the hospital, you are very similar to the other babies born that day. You've got almost everything in common with the neighbors on your street and around your city. You're not much different than the people in your country and around the globe. You were born a child of this world, but if you have come to faith in Christ, God is making you different than those other earthlings. He doesn't just forgive your sins to get your sorry self into heaven. He wants to display the glory of who He is through transforming your conduct and character. In fact, once you are saved, that transformation and *only that* is what the will of the Lord *IS*.

In 1 Thessalonians 5, Paul is rehearsing a list of specifics related to God's written will: **"Rejoice always, pray without ceasing, give thanks in all circumstances. . . . Do not quench the Spirit. Do not despise prophecies, but test everything; hold fast what is good"** (5:16–21). In the middle of it all he gives a wonderful summary statement: **"for this *IS* the will of God in Christ Jesus for you"** (emphasis mine). Get it? God's will for you *IS* about your behavior and His purpose in seeing it made more like His Son's. That's it, and the Bible does not teach that God's will *IS* any more or any less than that.

God uses hardship to shape and show our character. Christians go through the very same things that everyone else goes through. Christians get sick. Christians lose loved ones. Christians go through financial hardship. Christians suffer. God sees to it Himself, because He wants to display the splendor of who He is through the amazing, supernatural contrast between our lives and the lives of those who don't truly know Him. Sanctification is all about getting us ready for our star performance in the likeness of the **"morning star"** (Rev. 22:16), Jesus Christ. It's not about what happens to us but about how God sanctifies us to display how awesome He truly is. Of course we don't do this perfectly, but as true believers in Jesus who are experiencing His transforming power, we do it increasingly. This and only this *IS* God's will for us, which *IS* our sanctification.

People who get sidetracked searching for a blueprint God engineered about where to go to college and whom to marry lose a ton of traction looking for the plan instead of actually living. I hate this idea that there is a secret, perfect plan that God is super-cheap about revealing. This distorted, distracting concept hurts so many, gets insanely draining for people, and is not at all biblical. Again, 1 Thessalonians 4:3: **"For this is the will of God, your sanctification."** That's how God's will applies to your life and mine, and as God's Word conveys the specifics about how that looks, we are the new creation in

Christ; **"old things have passed away; behold, all things have become new"** (2 Cor. 5:17 NKJV).

God sanctifies His children through every relationship and life experience. Consider marriage, for example. Marriage is a laboratory for sanctification, the most intimate relationship in which your sharp edges are exposed and refined. God gives specific instructions regarding what His will *IS* for marriage. **"Husbands, love your wives, as Christ loved the church and gave himself up for her"** (Eph. 5:25). Husbands are to act like Christ, loving their wives in a sacrificial way. **"Wives, submit to your own husbands, as to the Lord"** (5:22). Wives are to respect their husbands, responding to their leadership as the church does to Christ. The way spouses give themselves to one another and the way they raise their family—all of this is spelled out in Scripture, part of what God's will *IS* for each of us as believers.

> Once we know what God wants us to know, it's time to get busy doing what God's will actually *IS*.

In fact, in life's most significant relationships, the problem isn't that God hasn't told us His will; the problem is that we struggle to embrace and obey it. Too often we plead to know God's will when in reality we are looking for relief from the commands to do His will, as revealed in the Bible. Behind many questions about God's will lurks a stubborn heart squirming to get off the hook. Isn't it true that because we find God's will in Scripture very difficult at times, we first make it opaque so we can be unclear about obedience? God doesn't give certain people a special pass to violate His will. Once we discover in Scripture the *how* of God's will for our behavior, it's time to get busy doing what God's will actually *IS*.

The Bible as Our Protection

From this point on, when we consider the concept of God's will, we must zero in exclusively on the Bible. Knowing now that the will of God *IS* the Word of God, we can make doing His will much simpler.

The guidelines in Scripture aren't meant to confine us; they protect us. God has surrounded our lives with His Word, like a fence around an open field. The fence is constructed from all of the truths written in the Bible. Within the fence are light and freedom; beyond the fence are darkness and danger. David described these moral confines of his life: **"The boundary lines have fallen for me in pleasant places; indeed, I have a beautiful inheritance"** (Ps. 16:6 csb). As long as you are living within the boundaries of God's Word, your life is going to be phenomenal. It will have direction and contentment.

Within the boundary lines, will we still have to deal with sin and pain? Yes, for we still live in a fallen world. But when we feel hurt, overwhelmed, or disillusioned in life, we can examine our decisions again. Did we choose based on God's Word, or did we assert our own will? When we choose to ignore the protection God offers within Scripture, we climb over the fence and into the darkness. Every time we disregard the Bible's guidelines, we can expect bad results.

Consider this in your own life. When you *have* experienced pain in life, how often has it been the result of choices you made that placed you outside the boundaries of God's Word? We are meant to live inside the protection of the Bible. God's sovereign will offers us abundant life within the protective borders of His Word.

Heavenly Father,

Thank You for creating me with a will of my own, for I'm created in Your image. Thank You for assuring me that You are the sovereign King over the universe, and nothing thwarts Your purposes. You use all things to advance Your kingdom. Thank You for revealing Your will through Your Word. Thank You that it's Your will for me to be both saved and sanctified, and that for the rest of my life, You will continue to refine me. I want to live like I belong to You, because I do. Father, give me the joy You reserve for those whose lives belong entirely to You. I yield myself and my will more completely to You, Lord, in the name of Jesus, my Savior and Redeemer. Amen.

CHAPTER 3

God's Exact Will for Me, Now?

IN THE PREVIOUS chapter we considered **God's sovereign will** (His master plan driving the universe and encompassing all of human history) and **His moral will**, or better phrased, **His written will** (God's plan for my personal behavior, as revealed in the Bible). But when people ask me about God's will, they are almost always wondering about God's so-called individual will. "What is God's will for my life?" they wonder.

I know the drill. Growing up, I was taught that God had an individual will for each one of us. In his classic book on God's will, *Decision Making and the Will of God*, Garry Friesen describes this concept as a dot—a very tiny, very specific dot, which represents God's will. Friesen's image of a dot is a genius illustration, showing how narrow and precarious and specific God's individual will has been painted by many well-meaning teachers of the Scriptures.[1]

"Find that tiny dot, James, and get on it. That's God's will for you." I was instructed to search for that dot in all my life choices. I was dispatched on the ultimate goose chase to discover God's will for the very street my exact house was on. Spending or vacation choices couldn't be off the dot. And once I was on the dot, I had to be vigilant not to climb or fall off without realizing it.

Very sincere Christians shackled me with this enslaving concept. Of course, they were just teaching me what they had been taught, but the problem with that teaching is it's requiring some strange rationalizations to believe even for a moment that I was actually on the dot. Sooner or later I made a bad choice and stepped off the dot. Growing up, I was taught that God had a perfect will (what He wanted) and a permissive will (what He allowed). Those two terms wrongly shaped and haunted my relationship with God. God's perfect will—that was the dot. If Christians consistently made the right choices—college, marriage, career, decision after decision after decision—then they were on the dot, in God's perfect will for them. People like D. L. Moody, Amy Carmichael, and Billy Graham stayed on the dot. They owned the dot! That's why their lives were so amazing, of course.

The rest of us, though, were kind of losers on some level. We made enough bad choices along the way that we were hopelessly off the dot. As a result, we became sort of spiritual vagrants, second-class Christians. Since we had ruined our own hopes for living in God's perfect will, we had to settle for what was called "God's permissive will." God would allow us to go on with our lives, though He was clearly disappointed because we did not find the dot and accomplish His "perfect will." In the back of our minds constantly was the awareness of God's enduring frown and look of apparent sadness with our frivolous wasting of perfect opportunity.

My perspective could be summarized in this short (not particularly award-winning) poem:

So sadly now, I'm off the dot.
I missed my chance, I lost the spot.
My life is stuck, pathetic lot.
Forever ruined! That's what I was taught.

Sometimes I wonder how many lives have been immobilized or even terrorized by such teaching. Does life feel like you have fallen and can't get up? Do you live in recurring fear that the next choice you make might be the wrong one that pushes you permanently off of God's "perfect plan" for you, which you're not all that sure you're on in the first place?

This "perfect will" teaching sounds holy, and it exalts the perfection of God's sovereign will. But if God's will for us is really that unknowable and undiscoverable, then we're just a single wrong choice away from total ruin. The false idea of God's perfect will is ludicrous when applied logically to a single life choice, such as marriage. When I was in college, I started doing the math and noticed a big problem when I focused on the whole matter of choosing a life partner. If there is only one perfect, lifetime partner in God's will for each of us, and you have to find that chosen person, then what happens if you make the wrong choice? If there's only one possible right choice, it's conceivable that some of us will make the wrong choice and marry a person God does not will us to marry. And then, God forbid, you and your wrong spouse have kids. Those kids were never supposed to exist. Meanwhile, the person you were supposed to marry is married to someone else, and they're having kids who were never supposed to exist either. (Does God have a will for people who weren't supposed to exist?) Now imagine those kids are all grown up. They have nobody to marry—they're not even supposed to be here! Then one day you're in a restaurant and see some kids and suddenly have this vague feeling that they were supposed to be your kids. The whole thing is absurd. In a generation or two, God's perfect will would be only a distant memory of an imagined possibility. The arrangement does not make sense, but people try to live their lives this way. Searching in vain for a dot that doesn't exist is not how God wants us to live, nor does it in any way approximate what God's will actually *IS*.

> In a generation or two, God's perfect will would be only a distant memory of an imagined possibility.

Worst of all, instead of figuring out that marriage is hard work, some people decide, "I must have married the wrong person. I think maybe this person isn't God's will for me. I may need to get out of this marriage to get back on the dot." That thinking is so dangerous and wrong, as it invites us to climb over the fence of God's will, only to find we have entered a dark wilderness. Nothing good comes from believing God has a specific, precise, individual will, and it's not in any way biblical.

God's will for you in a difficult marriage is to keep the commitments you made, even when it's painful to do so. God commends the one **"who swears to his own hurt and does not change"** (Ps. 15:4). God's will for you is to spend the rest of your life with that person you chose, come hell or high water, good times or bad times. That's your person for the rest of your life. Get your eyes off other options, get your eyes back on your lifetime partner, and spend the rest of your life honoring and glorifying God by making that marriage everything that it can possibly be. The grass isn't greener over the fence; the grass is greener where you water it, and that *IS* God's will for you. Pull the weeds and tend to the grass of your own marriage. Jesus made a very narrow, very specific provision for divorce, and it applies to a sliver of the population. If you're hurting or in doubt, see a Christian pastor or counselor. Otherwise, be assured that God's will *IS* your sanctification through this trial.

Because I pastor a church filled with twenty-first-century human beings, I know all about the ravages of divorce and the forces undermining marriage today. I realize that, for some readers, the paragraphs above provoke pain, hopelessness, even anger. You may already feel beaten down. Your marriage (in some cases, marriages) may be long past. But the future lies before you. Wherever you find yourself today, I encourage you to discover how to live in God's will going forward. For those with painful pasts, you may have to work through some hard feelings first. You may realize you have been formulating or carrying out some plans for your marriage that are definitely outside God's written will. Remember that inside the boundaries of the Bible you will find blessing. The whispers from outside the fence invite you to darkness and self-destruction, reaping negative consequences for your choices and forfeiting God's blessing. Stay in the protection of God's written will. Trust me, despite the difficulties you'll face, God's will *IS* always best.

> Remember that inside the boundaries of the Bible you will find blessing.

Meanwhile, we have to reject the idea that there's a perfect someone out there. There is no perfect mate! Think about your own level of perfection. Could you ever be perfect for someone? The whole concept of a "perfect match" places unrealistic expectations on a marriage relationship, which neither you nor your mate can fulfill. This is such a destructive teaching because it ignores the truth that every marriage is made up of two flawed, sinful human beings. A marriage is a work in progress with two people who are works in progress. Wedding vows include the phrase "for better or for worse" for a reason, even if the bride and groom are in a haze at that moment. Life includes both better and worse!

The false concept of a perfect mate is also destructive because it takes what is basically the world's idealized, romantic approach to marriage and tries to give it a spiritual stamp of approval. If falling in love is a sure route to marital bliss, then it can be tempting to reason, "It's God's will that I fell for you." Yet it's scary how often I hear Christians who are already married say things like this about people other than their spouses. Too many people get married today without seriously weighing what will be required to grow together and to be faithful for sixty or more years.

If this idea of the perfect mate, handpicked for you by God, is so off, then why do many Christians buy into it? Because they select certain passages of Scripture and make them universal. For example, in Genesis 24, the Lord supernaturally led Abraham's servant Eliezer to a specific bride for Isaac from his family tree (Rebekah). Another widely used biblical passage is Acts 16:6–10, in which the apostle Paul received a very specific, supernatural call to leave Asia and go to Macedonia. Well-meaning people read these descriptions of

God's *specific* guidance and try to make them *normative*—as if this is the way it's supposed to happen for everyone about everything. Yet the reason these accounts are in the Bible is because they were so unusual. This kind of supernatural direction is not the normal pattern for life—even the lives of the characters in these stories. Paul did not wait for a vision before he made other travel plans. And Eliezer approached his task to find a wife for Isaac with a mixture of wisdom, prayer, fleece, and caution. The lessons we apply from the stories in the Bible must be developed carefully. Too often students of the Bible take subjects where "the Bible reports" and wrongly make them into "the Bible exhorts." The Bible often *describes* but does not *prescribe* certain actions on the part of God or His people. It tells us what people did, what God did, and what happened as a result. But it seldom promises the same results if we simply imitate those Bible characters. (Otherwise, people who want to imitate the Genesis 24 story would have to commission their parents to choose a third party, elderly man to take a long road trip on a camel in order to find them a bride. Anyone interested?) The Bible is packed with wisdom, but gleaning binding precepts from particular stories requires faithful study and examination of the historic understanding and application of that passage. The scriptural context influences how we apply the stories of the Bible, not to mention the totality of Scripture versus the single passage "private interpretation" Peter condemns (2 Pet. 1:20–21).

God as Micromanager?

Looking back on my own life, I see now that I grew up in a spiritual environment that promoted the "individualized" will of God. When I first started to question the teaching and read the more recent challenges to this historic interpretive error, I instinctively felt I was off base—maybe even off the dot! I had memorized several Bible passages that were used as a basis for the confident claim that God had a detailed blueprint for each of our lives. But when I actually studied these passages, I discovered that the view of God's will they were being used to teach was far from what the verses actually meant. How had I missed this?

Let's look together at five of those passages that confuse people about whether God has an individualized will for our lives. One or more of these may have already come to mind in defense of the idea that God has a detailed, specific will for your life.

Just so we're very clear before we examine the Scriptures, I do not believe that God has an individual will for each person. God did not write a personalized, divine, paint-by-number pattern for each of us to find and follow. I am not convinced there is an exact place where you are meant to work or a specific home address God wrote into His special plan for you. God does not have some top secret, individualized code you should be cracking to get your life on plan.

God's will is about the kind of person you were, the kind of person you currently are, and the kind of person you can become. Within the parameters of the Bible (the protective

> God's will is about the kind of person you were, the kind of person you currently are, and the kind of person you can become.

fence His Word raises around your life), He leaves a lot of the choices up to you. God is glorified when you make good decisions based on His broad directives.

And now, let's explore five passages used to support the claim that God has an individual will for each of us.

1) Path or No Path?

Here's the first pillar of God's so-called individual will:

Trust in the LORD with all your heart, and do not lean on your own understanding. In all your ways acknowledge him, and he will make straight your paths (Prov. 3:5–6).

Caution! Handle with care! This is a beloved passage for many Christians (including me). Huge throngs of people have chosen Proverbs 3:5–6 as their life verses. Some even engraved the King James Version on their memories as children: **"Trust in the LORD with all thine heart; and lean not unto thine**

own understanding. In all thy ways acknowledge him, and he shall direct thy paths." Inspiring verses, right?

Yet often misquoted and misunderstood. I have heard these verses twisted in various forms, such as this: "See, there's the path. It's a series of dots, and I have to be on a dot in the path specifically laid out for my life. I must make the right choices. We're going out for dinner tonight. I feel like I want Chinese food, but maybe we should go for Italian. It's a tough choice. I'm just trying to discern exactly what God wants me to do at every single bend in the road."

Is God really a controlling micromanager? No. God doesn't have an opinion about where you go for dinner! Go to the place you can afford. Go to the place your spouse likes best. We can get so caught up in constantly measuring, analyzing, and fretting over God's will, but that's not God's attitude at all when it comes to our lives.

Consider the final phrase: **"and he shall direct thy paths"** (KJV). When the NIV translation committee was laboring over the translation of this passage, the scholars were startled to discover that the Hebrew wording did not support the traditional notion of God directing our paths. Instead, the wording more precisely translated to **"and he will make your paths straight"** (NIV), nearly identical to the ESV, **"and he will make straight your paths."**

Proverbs 3:5–6 is not teaching that there's a path of dots that you had better get on or your life is going to be a travesty.

The passage is saying that if you trust in God with your whole heart (when you are making decisions), don't lean on your own understanding (when you are making decisions), and acknowledge God in every decision you make, He will make your paths straight. The assumption is not that you have to know or even guess His will before you make decisions, because the Lord will make sure you don't take any deadly detours. Even when life is difficult, you won't be wasting your time. Even when life is painful, you won't just be marking off days on the calendar. God promises that your path will be straight. He retains the right to intervene and adjust (straighten) your course, but He also gives you plenty of room to obey. No wasted steps, no wasted anything. God will guide and lead you so that your life unfolds in such a way that His highest purposes are accomplished in you. None of this depends on where you work or live. God's highest purposes are about the kind of person you are. This *IS* the will of God— your sanctification.

> The Lord will make sure you don't take any deadly detours.

2) Which Way Is the Right Way?

Here's a second pillar of the individualized view of God's will:

And though the Lord give you the bread of adversity and the water of affliction, yet your Teacher will not hide himself anymore, but your eyes shall see your Teacher. And your ears shall hear a word behind you, saying, "This is the way, walk in it," when you turn to the right or when you turn to the left (Isa. 30:20–21).

These are actually the theme verses for Walk in the Word, the radio and television ministry I'm privileged to lead. Again, inspiring verses—often misquoted. "See," some people say, "God has a specific, turn-by-turn plan for our lives. God will tell us the exact way to walk."

Consider the context. These words were written by the prophet Isaiah during the reign of King Ahaz. All of God's other spokespeople had gone into hiding, afraid for their lives, but God was working through Isaiah's ministry. As people responded to God's discipline and returned to Him, they were given this promise: **"Yet your teachers will not be moved into a corner anymore, But your eyes shall see your teachers"** (Isa. 30:20 NKJV). The confusion comes over a capital letter. Some translations use "Teacher," singular and capitalized, suggesting the verse is talking about God. The capitalization is not in the original language, so the more accurate translation is **"teachers,"** plural and lower case, referring to God's servants. The point is that God will raise up people in your life to communicate His truth to you so that you will have wisdom in making decisions that honor Him. God provides teachers!

Life includes a continual cascade of decisions. The older you get, the more you realize how much life is directed by choices. Does God care about the big decisions in life? Absolutely! Does He provide resources to help us make wise decisions? Yes! Does He have a singular, detailed, specific plan for every decision, including those between equally good alternatives? No. He generously lets us choose. He wants us to choose what we want, as long as we want His will, which *IS* His Word.

> The older you get, the more you realize how much life is directed by choices.

3) Am I Filled with God's Will?

The third pillar supporting the idea of God's individual will is apparently found here:

And so, from the day we heard, we have not ceased to pray for you, asking that you may be filled with the knowledge of his will in all spiritual wisdom and understanding (Col. 1:9).

Case closed? Does the phrase **"filled with the knowledge of his will"** imply that God has an individualized will for each of us? The next verse gives us a vital context clue: **"so as to walk in a manner worthy of the Lord, fully pleasing to him, bearing fruit in every good work and increasing in the knowledge of God"** (Col. 1:10). Ah-ha! That *IS* God's will for us, which is the same for all of His children, as revealed in Scripture. God's will for you is not some specific, detailed blueprint. It's about the kind of person you are—reflecting more and more the character qualities of His Son, Jesus Christ. That is what Paul prays for the Colossian believers to truly understand.

4) Is God's Will Perfect?

Pillar four comes from Romans 12:1–2:

I appeal to you therefore, brothers, by the mercies of God, to present your bodies as a living sacrifice, holy and acceptable to God, which is your spiritual worship. Do not be conformed to this world, but be transformed by the renewal of your mind, that by testing you may discern what is the will of God, what is good and acceptable and perfect.

In this classic passage, the apostle Paul shifts from doctrine (Rom. 1–11) to practice (Rom. 12–16). These two verses mark a theological transition. What *IS* the will of God? To **"present your bodies as a living sacrifice"** and to **"be**

transformed by the renewal of your mind." Is His will specific? Yes. Is it individualized? No. It requires a constant series of choices with Him in mind, not a step by step life assembly booklet. God's will for you *IS* about the kind of person you are.

> Is His will specific? Yes. Is it individualized? No.

If you are the kind of person God wants you to be, the kind of person He is growing you into, then you will make the right decisions that please and honor Him.

5) What Is God's Will?

The fifth and final faulty pillar most commonly used to defend this frustrating and unbiblical view of God's will is found in Ephesians 5:15–17:

> **Look carefully then how you walk, not as unwise but as wise, making the best use of the time, because the days are evil. Therefore do not be foolish, but understand what the will of the Lord is.**

This passage underscores the same point as the other four: *God's will IS about who we are.* The idea of an individual will—demanding of ourselves and others a perspective that sees every moment of life preprogrammed by God—makes for miserable, paranoid living rather than joyous, wise living in the glorious freedom of what His will actually *IS*.

Implications

Those five, treasured, biblical passages have often been misinterpreted, forced to hold up the false idea that God has a highly specific, individualized will for our lives. If we knock down those five pillars, then the whole structure begins to crumble. In the clear light of day, we can see that those beloved verses actually show us that God's will *IS* about who we are as His children.

So what? What are the implications of taking our decision-making role seriously? We're not just trying to guess what God wants us to choose in every situation; we're actually exercising a God-given responsibility.

Here's an important qualification. God does have some specific things He wants His individual children to do. He surely has moments in life where He wants to guide our steps, keep us from stumbling, and lead us to a meaningful role in life we can fulfill. But His guidance doesn't sound like, "This and nothing else, so you'd better figure it out or all is lost!" If God has a specific task He wants you to do, then He will reveal it to you in a very obvious way. He will let you know, "I want you to talk to her about Me. I want you to move back to your hometown and help the church you grew up in. I want you to _____." If God wants you to do something, He will reveal it to you in a very obvious way. When God's people give themselves to living wisely, making real and wise choices based on God's Word, then God will take care of the very occasional points of particular guidance. While God does have specific things He wants His children to do, by far, *by far, by far,* God has left most choices up to us.

The Scriptures make some choices explicitly clear, and our decisions on those matters should be no-brainers. For example, should you lie? If you face a situation at work in which the easy, tempting strategy would be to say something false or twist the truth, a tactic that seems to be working for others, should you lie? What is God's will for you on this choice? Easy decision. God has given us a clear "no" on lying, so which part of God's "no" don't we understand?

Other tests of God's will occur in everyday life. Should you take something that doesn't belong to you (otherwise known as stealing)? The fact that God included **"You shall not steal"** in the ten cardinal rules we call the Ten Commandments should clue us in clearly to what God wants (Exod. 20:15). Should you covet, longing for something your friend or neighbor or coworker has? Again, clear choice (20:17).

But what do you do when the choices and alternatives are not clear? What do you do when the choice is not a matter of a clear, biblical mandate that distinguishes right and wrong?

What do you do when your decision is not prescribed within God's Word?

When handling equal choices, God wants you to make the choice that would please you. God loves you. My mother, now with the Lord, was a generous and kind woman, and she often baked treats for my brothers and me. Now imagine she offered me three different kinds of cookies and said, "Here, James, I made you fresh-baked goodies. Would you like chocolate chip, peanut butter, or oatmeal raisin?" Would she be thinking to herself, *He'd better figure out that I want him to take the oatmeal raisin! If he chooses chocolate chip, I'm going to be disappointed?* No, my mom would want me to choose the one I wanted. She would be pleased by the fact that I enjoyed what she labored to create.

God doesn't care so much about the place you live or the car you drive, as long as you can afford it and you're using it to honor Him. These are the decisions God has freely given us to make. Later we will look more closely at how to make decisions that honor the Lord and His Word.

Within the boundaries of God's Word, we find structure, direction, protection, and freedom. There are various, valid choices within God's will. We don't have to live in terror of making a mistake and violating His purposes. When painful things happen to us, we don't have to immediately conclude that we're being punished for being off the dot or that God's will is callously arbitrary. A child born with a disability is not

God's idea of a special test for parents, nor is it a punishment for parents who are off the dot.

No, the world is a fallen, sinful place where unspeakably bad things happen. The creation itself is cursed. Bad things happen to "good" people, and God does allow those things within His sovereign will. But to see God as directly causing every point of pain is an affront to the loving kindness of God. God promises His grace and Himself, and that's enough for us. When painful things happen, we should never let someone isolate a few verses about sovereignty and fashion them into God's directly casting our pain upon us. Yes, He is sovereign over it, and yes, He could have prevented it (and no doubt often does). But no, He did not push someone's kid out in front of a bus because He wants the parents to be better Christians.

> God promises His grace and Himself, and that's enough for us.

What about the Past?

And now to the issue of past sins, mistakes, and bad decisions that some of you may be wondering about. No matter what wrong choices you have made, you have not missed God's best for the rest of your life. Though we know the past, we need not dwell on it. When the past is in God's hands, through confession and forgiveness, we can set our sights on walking according to God's will today and tomorrow. We can echo Paul: **"Brothers, I do not consider that I have made it my own. But one thing I do: forgetting what lies behind and straining forward to what lies ahead, I press on toward the goal for the prize of the upward call of God in Christ Jesus"** (Phil. 3:13–14).

Having written that, I know who's reading these words—people like me. You've said things and done things and made choices you deeply regret. If you could live your life over again, if you could go back, you would do some things differently. Is that true of you? If only I could go back, I would do some things so differently. Under the traditional view of God's individualized will, the best I could hope for would be a shadow life of limited use to God. But that perspective completely discounts the reality of God's forgiveness and power. When we resist God's sovereign will (which is impossible in the end) and mishandle His revealed will (the Bible), it's easy to pursue a fragile, individualized will of God that we shatter almost immediately. In that contest of wills, we never win—it's only a matter of time until we end up losing. In this model, our decisions ruin God's carefully laid plans and reveal that He's actually helpless to do much about it. The individualized view of God leaves us with a fragmented and woefully distorted idea of God Himself, who's at the mercy of our choices.

Instead of trying to pick up the broken pieces of your past life, you can know God's blessing, favor, and grace upon the rest of your life. Family patterns that have affected you can be broken in the next generation. Your children can grow up far beyond what you may have been and accomplish things for God that you never dreamed of. Do you see? Our God is so great that He works with our choices. We participate in His will! He takes our choices and actions and still works out His sovereign will. How freeing! We don't have to live under the constant threat of ruining God's plan for our lives. Instead, we can experience God's fullest blessing upon the rest of our lives.

Meet the Shepherd-Guide

This marks a major shift for many of us. We need to clarify how we think of God in our day-to-day decisions. Too many of us actually treat God as a helpless sovereign who came up with a perfect personal plan for us a long time ago and now worries and sighs over how often we mess it up. That's not how God introduces Himself to us in the Bible. He is more ingenious, involved, and invincible than our weak mental image of Him.

Is God the hand-wringing, secretive puppet master? No.

God has revealed Himself to us as our Shepherd-Guide. Come with me again to Isaiah 40. The first few verses in Isaiah 40 describe the scope of God's sovereign will. It's a glimpse into what happens when God decides to intervene in history. Everything falls into place. Eventually everything yields to Him. Highways become straight. Uneven ground becomes level. The rough places become a plain, and the glory of the Lord is revealed (Isa. 40:3–4). That's God's sovereign will.

The next verses reveal God's will for our lives. **"The grass withers, the flower fades, but the word of our God will stand forever"** (40:8). Through His written will, the Bible, God reveals the parts of His sovereign will He wants us to know and states the guidelines by which we can order our lives.

But notice how Isaiah describes the way God guides our lives: **"He will tend his flock like a shepherd; he will gather the lambs in his arms; he will carry them in his bosom, and gently lead those that are with young"** (40:11). Do we want to know how God leads and guides us? Do we long to see how His will intersects with our lives? God relates to His children the way a good Shepherd relates to His sheep.

When life is hardest, when circumstances are most difficult, when we feel the deepest pain, is God there? Absolutely! Is He tenderly guiding, gathering, leading, and carrying us? Always!

What kind of a shepherd would say to his sheep, "Listen up! We're going out into the pasture now. Don't eat off the wrong tuft of grass. I've designated certain blades of grass for each of you. That's the only grass I want you to eat. The pasture may look delicious, but I want you to focus on which grass to eat"? Yet that is exactly how many of us have perceived God and His so-called individualized, highly restrictive, almost cryptic will. As the Bible so accurately describes, we are all like sheep that have gone astray (Isa. 53:6). We are bent by nature to run outside the boundary that God has generously provided, but our Shepherd keeps leading us back and **"He makes [us] lie down in green pastures"** (Ps. 23:2).

A loving Shepherd would never paralyze His sheep with fear over where to rest, and that's not God's heart for you. Once you are safely inside the pasture of God's Word, God leaves the choices up to you. As long as you don't jump over the fence, you are free to choose within its protection. You have genuine decisions you can make inside the green pasture of His written will for you. When you ask serious questions about choices in your life, you can seek to follow scriptural directives, but don't fret over a highly individualized and easily missed series of predetermined decisions you figure out precisely *or else*.

Doesn't following a Shepherd-Guide sound like a more joyful life than following a divine architect who hides the blueprint and leaves us guessing in the dark? And being a Christ-follower is meant to be a joyful endeavor. As Jesus told us, **"The thief comes only to steal and kill and destroy. I came that they may have life and have it abundantly"** (John 10:10). Yet how many of us get around to enjoying the abundant life Jesus promised? Many of us feel as if it's sinful to enjoy things, while others of us are squinting so hard, searching for the dot, that we're missing the good all around us. While we never want to set our hearts on our stuff, we would do well to set our hearts on God and enjoy His gifts. **"As for the rich in this present age, charge them not to be haughty, nor to set their hopes on the uncertainty of riches, but on God, who richly provides us with everything to enjoy"** (1 Tim. 6:17).

Father God,

Thank You for being my Shepherd-Guide. Thank You for how You gently tend and lead me. So often I act like a sheep who is hovering over the succulent grass You provided, continually looking back at You to ask, "Can I eat this? Can I chew on this blade of grass?" Please help me to have greater confidence in Your gifts and guidance. Help me to live more fully the abundant life You provided for me through Your Son, Jesus Christ, in whose matchless name I pray. Amen.

CHAPTER 4

Does God Have Specifics for Me?

ARE YOU ONE of those curious readers who skip ahead in the book or read the last chapter first? If you flipped directly to this chapter because of the title, then you will need the context of the first three chapters. Or maybe you're the student in class who always appreciates when the teacher does a brief review so you feel oriented to the new material. Since we're exploring such an in-depth topic, let's do a quick review together before we consider the next angles.

Does God have a sovereign will? Yes, He absolutely does. God has a secret plan, which controls the outcome of all matters in the universe. The Bible assures us, **"In him we have obtained an inheritance, having been predestined according to the purpose of him who works all things according**

to the counsel of his will" (Eph. 1:11). Nothing and no one thwarts the purposes of God. He is in ultimate control of time and space. God holds the overriding veto, which all of us, with our limited decision-making power, must eventually acknowledge. We can resist God's sovereignty, but we never win. The list of those who have staged failed coups is long—kings and queens, presidents, rulers, rebels, revolutionaries, you, and I—but none of us can prevent God's sovereign purposes from being accomplished. God's sovereign parade of His ultimate purposes is in formation, marching in time and on time, with perfection.

In fact, God accomplishes His sovereign will with His feet up. Neither creating nor maintaining the universe strains God. He isn't awake at night worrying. He could rule a thousand universes like ours and not be taxed or tired in any way. God's power is infinite, and His sovereignty is supreme. He is constantly working out His purposes in this universe. That's His sovereign will.

Does God have a moral will? Yes. In fact, the moral will of God *IS* the Word of God. God's moral will and God's Word are one and the same. That's why I recommend referring to God's moral will as His written will—because it's written for us in His Word! God's sovereign will is God's business, but He has made His Word our business. It's the prescription for life that God has revealed to us. In the Bible, God teaches us what to believe and how to live.

When God gives us directions, they come in the form of commands, not suggestions. He doesn't preface His rules with soft disclaimers: "Dear children, you might want to think about this." His prescriptions for life are framed confidently: "I'm God; you're not. Trust Me—I made you, I love you, and I know how you function best, so do this!" God isn't casual, cautious, or uncertain about what He tells us to do.

When we hear that God has given some clear-cut commandments, many of us don't like it. This is particularly true when God's commandments cramp our style. We respond with an instinctive, "Well, who does He think He is?" Some of us have learned to get over that first reaction in a hurry. The better we know God, the more we can accept what He tells us to do.

Our obedience to God's Word shows our love for Him. **"And by this we know that we have come to know him, if we keep his commandments. Whoever says 'I know him' but does not keep his commandments is a liar, and the truth is not in him, but whoever keeps his word, in him truly the love of God is perfected. By this we may know that we are in him: whoever says he abides in him ought to walk in the same way in which [Jesus] walked"** (1 John 2:3–6). God's will was personified by Jesus, who lived a perfect life before dying as an atoning sacrifice for our sins. So how do we know what God's will looks like? Through the example of Jesus and the teaching of Scripture. The Bible teaches . . .

how to be forgiven and saved,

how to walk closely with God,

how to worship, pray, and read His Word,

how to train your children,

how to manage your finances,

how to have a loving, life-giving marriage for life,

how and where to serve to be part of God's kingdom purposes (hint: church),

how to resolve conflict and get past the wounds and disappointments of life,

and every other how-to that pertains to life and godliness (2 Pet. 1:3).

It is striking to note, though, what's missing from that how-to list: God's Word never teaches us how to know God's will. Though the Bible reveals God's guidelines on how to live, God's Word does not teach us how to know His will. Nowhere in the Bible can we find a set of directions, a process, or a system that decodes God's specific will for a situation. This is an important distinction. Unless you are obeying a direct command in Scripture, it's never a good idea to explain a decision by saying, "It's God's will that I do this." Christians should respect God's will too highly to attach His authority and weight to our decisions by calling them "God's will." (Much more on this later.)

In fact, "What is God's will for my life?" is a question we are never told to ask in Scripture. The subject does not even come up. Why not? Because, as we have been explaining, it is rooted in the widely taught but mistaken view that God has a specific, individual will for every one of us.

Does God have an individualized, customized, itemized will for your life? No. God does not have an undisclosed, detailed blueprint for your life. There's no secret, unwritten code that specifies how you are to choose, how you are to act, and how you are to move in every particular situation. God's will *IS* about the kind of person you are, not which street you live on or where you're supposed to get your paycheck. God's will *IS* about being a certain quality of person.

In the last chapter, we tried to obliterate the dot theory[2] of God's will—that there's a perfect spot called God's will, and you'd better get on it. If you make a wrong decision, you'll be caught off the dot. Thinking of God's will this way is terribly stressful. It would be as if someone told you that God really wants you to watch yourself fall asleep. In fact, it's the only way He'll be happy with you. If you miss that

> God does not have an undisclosed, detailed blueprint for your life.

moment when you fall asleep, you'll regret it. Now of course, that would be a ridiculous dilemma: either you watch yourself and don't go to sleep, or you go to sleep and don't watch yourself.

The dot theory induces that same brand of stress, as if it's impossible to please God. Either you practice what God has revealed in His Word about His will and don't worry about what you don't know, or you spend all your time worrying about what you don't know about God's will and never get around to doing all of His will that He's revealed in His Word! I don't know about you, but I want to be like Jesus. His greatest joy, His **"food,"** was doing His Father's will. **"My food is to do the will of him who sent me and to accomplish his work"** (John 4:34). Jesus didn't have the dot theory in mind. In the Gospels, we never see Him laboring over a decision, wringing His hands over God's will in that particular moment. No, He was too busy fulfilling God's will by loving those around Him.

The quest to know God's individual will is not commanded, illustrated, or commended in the Scriptures. That quest causes a lot of pain and heartache in the lives of well-meaning believers.

People stuck on or confused by the dot have one last trump card: Jeremiah 29:11. In addition to those passages we studied in the previous chapter, many Christians are inspired (and confused) by Jeremiah 29:11. **"For I know the plans I have for you, declares the LORD, plans for welfare and not for evil, to give you a future and a hope."** What a beloved verse!

The argument goes like this: "Well, surely this verse teaches that God has a specific, individual will for every one of us." (How self-aggrandizing it must sound to God to hear us applying verses about the covenant with His chosen people at the ultimate moment in their history to a decision like, "Should I take the promotion and move to Toledo?") Let's break this passage down a bit and look closely at it together.

That opening phrase, **"For I know the plans I have for you, declares the LORD,"** sounds very direct. Some literal translations read, **"For I know the thoughts that I think toward you, says the LORD"** (NKJV). The word often translated **"plans"** refers to thoughts about the future. When we read **"plans,"** we might interpret that to mean minutely spelled out details involving every decision the children of Israel would make in their lives—and by application, possibly the same details related to our own lives. Unfortunately, that's how many people read and misapply it. Note again the **"plans"** or **"thoughts"** God has toward His children. They're actually not specific plans but fairly general and linked to how we relate to Him.

What are God's thoughts about our future? We don't have to wonder what His plans are; He tells us: **"plans for welfare and not for evil, to give you a future and a hope."** Note the broad boundaries of the wonderful, lush pasture of freedom to choose, not a specific, detailed, just-for-you plan. But God doesn't stop there. He goes on: **"Then you will call upon me and come and pray to me, and I will hear you. You will seek**

me and find me, when you seek me with all your heart. I will be found by you, declares the LORD, and I will restore your fortunes and gather you from all the nations and all the places where I have driven you, declares the LORD, and I will bring you back to the place from which I sent you into exile" (Jer. 29:12–14). In the context, God was declaring that the former days of His people's rebellion would not be the end of the story. He was offering to give fresh grace to every rebellious son and daughter who would truly lean in to Him in fresh, intentional ways. He makes the very same promise to you and me today. He doesn't have a land for us; that was unique to the situation. He promises to respond to our seeking Him the way He responds to all of His children, and that is truly awesome. These are God's plans for your future—not to "find His will" but to find Him! When you seek Him with all your heart, you will find Him. This passage describes some of the blessings that come from a dynamic, intimate, growing relationship with the Lord.

> These are God's plans for your future—not to "find His will" but to find Him!

We are tempted to believe that God's plans for us are about where we should live and what car we should drive. Those are our plans, related to our desires and preferences. We have to stop trying to get God on our program. Too many of us pray until we're convinced that God's will is for us to do what we wanted to do all along! What's worse than a misguided Christian setting sail for certain danger, backing off all objection to the contrary by declaring, "We have prayed about it and believe it's God's will"? What about God's revealed will in how to listen to counsel and heed the warnings of those in authority over us?

God Has a Dream

God's dream for your future is not that He would somehow get on your program. God's dream for your future *IS* that you would get on His program. God doesn't dream about where you're going to live or what kind of decision you're going to make about your vacation or some silly minutia. God's dreams for your future are about an amazing intimacy with Him that you have not yet experienced.

God continually calls us deeper and deeper into the fullness of life in Him. God envisions a day when what matters most to you is unrelated to the trappings of life (which you may have been tempted to refer to as God's will for your life) but instead relates to Him! God's will for you *IS* a vertical relationship where those things become less and less important as you are caught up into the depth and glowing height of knowing and loving the Lord. (If you crave more evidence, take a moment to read Ephesians 3:14–19 in a fresh, new way.) That's what eternity is going to be all about. God longs for us to seek Him and find Him because we search for Him with all of our heart.

Jeremiah 29:11 absolutely does not teach that there's a detailed blueprint about your future that God is waiting for you to figure out. Yes, God has a sovereign will. Yes, God has guidelines for our behavior (the Bible). But no, God does not have a specific, detailed plan for each individual.

> Jeremiah 29:11 absolutely does not teach that there's a detailed blueprint about your future that God is waiting for you to figure out.

This is good news! For some of us, it's a cosmic shift to reject the traditional view of God's will and embrace the idea that God's will *IS* about who we are. After we realign our thinking according to God's Word, we can expect some clear, distinct benefits, otherwise known as *blessings,* in our lives. What will happen if we take a biblical approach to practicing the will of God as opposed to worrying about whether or not we've really "found" our personalized version of His will?

Embrace What God's Will *IS*
and Count Your Blessings

Blessing #1: We can conform our beliefs to the teaching of Scripture.

Since there are no Bible passages that connect the phrase "the will of God" to personal life decisions, we won't make decisions as if there were. There are no Bible passages that connect the matter of God's will directly to where to go to college, what spouse to choose, what job to take, what house to buy, what vacation to go on, or even the number of children to have. In fact, there are no Bible passages that teach or encourage us to discover God's will at all! Every time

> For some of us, it's a cosmic shift to reject the traditional view of God's will and embrace the idea that God's will *IS* about who we are.

the phrase "the will of God" or "God's will" is used in Scripture, the passages are talking about either the sovereign will of God or the behavioral guidelines of God's Word that are incumbent upon every Christ-follower.

Do you want to be blessed and have a successful life? Do you want to be prosperous in the biblical sense of the word? Conform your thinking and acting and believing to what God's Word actually says. James tells it to us straight: **"But** be doers of the word, and not hearers only, deceiving your-selves" (James 1:22). We have plenty of God's Word to keep us busy every day of our lives.

Blessing #2: We can live free from anxiety and guilt about God's will.

What could cause more stress, anxiety, and guilt than praying for something that doesn't even exist? What seems like God's radio silence is actually His letting you choose.

Let's say that you are looking for a job and suddenly receive three job offers. After thanking God, you might be tempted to ask, "Which one, God, which one? Please, God, tell me which one am I supposed to take!" Instead of thanking God for three possibilities, you may end up resenting God for complicating your life. But if God doesn't have an individualized will that requires you to choose one particular job, then what happens next? You get to make a decision.

Let's say you look carefully at the three job opportunities. You practice due diligence and take a closer look at the company cultures. Perhaps you discover that one of the employers may expect you to do some things that seem a little shady. From reading the job description or from talking to other employees, you can sense that you will be pressured to lie or distort the truth in this job. Is that God's will for you? No. So that job's out. By simply applying what God has already revealed in His

Word, you didn't need a divine neon sign pointing to that job that reads, "Don't take this one! It's a trap!"

So now you are down to two job options. They seem fairly equal on all fronts: pay, commute, advancement opportunities. Both seem to use your gifts and abilities well. Which job should you choose? Whichever one you want.

While there are many personal factors you should consider in the decision, you should not ask, "What on earth is God's will about this?" Christian friends may ask, "Are you sure this is God's will for you?" This taps into the fear that motivates much of our fretting over decisions. You can confidently answer, "What I realized is that it's God's will for me to make good and wise decisions and that His sovereign will is able to handle what I have decided."

There are two primary reasons God usually doesn't answer the prayer, "What's Your will about this decision, Lord?" It's definitely not because He doesn't want you to know. God either doesn't answer that prayer because 1) He has already answered in His Word, or 2) He has given you the choice.

It's not that God doesn't care about the decision you make. He cares very much about your decision. I love David's description in Psalm 31: **"For you are my rock and my fortress; and for your name's sake you lead me and guide me . . . and you have not delivered me into the hand of the enemy; you have set my feet in a broad place"** (31:3, 8).

What good news! God has not set your feet in a cramped, little place, like a narrow ledge with a sharp drop-off on either side. God has set your feet in a large, comfortable place. You are not in danger of falling off with God. You're not in danger of accidentally stepping off the dot and missing God's best and His blessing for your life.

When we face decisions, we can follow the pattern of Proverbs 3:5–6: trust God, lean on more than just our own understanding, and acknowledge Him as we choose. We're not stuck in a holding pattern until God finally lets us know which choice He secretly wants us to make.

Blessing #3: We can recognize the validity of equal options.

Sometimes we get two or more options, and they're all good ones. How phenomenal that God would bless us with equal options. It doesn't matter which we choose. We can choose the one we like. God does not hide behind every choice to see if we make a wise decision, hoping to trap us in a mistake. God is excited to unfold His sovereign plan that incorporates our decisions, even if we do not fully understand how. Sometimes there are equally good options.

In the traditional view of God's individualized will, there's one house you're supposed to buy and one house you're not supposed to buy, and you had better figure it out and not buy the wrong house. In the biblical view of God's will, either of the houses may be fine. God will use you on either street. In either place, life will be a mixture of wonderful and hard.

In the traditional view of God's will, we agonize, "Which car is it, Lord? I can't decide. I know You have one in mind; show me, God." Back and forth, back and forth, crying out to God, "Lord, is it the Ford or the Chevy? Which car do I choose? Should it be blue or white?" Could it be that God's will for somebody is a blue vehicle? Forget all that. We can relax and recognize the validity of equal options.

Blessing #4: We can challenge immature or unwise decisions of loved ones—and be open to having our own decisions challenged.

This gets to the heart of the matter. If God does have an individual will for me, then who decides what His individual will is? I do. And I get to frame my choices with the indisputable claim, "This is God's will." With that pronouncement, how can I give permission to wise people in my life to question what I have called "God's will"? Putting my decisions in the "God's will" category removes them from objection. The problem is that when you give anyone, yourself or someone else, a way to make unchallengeable decisions, it will lead to chaos and eventual isolation in your life.

When I was in college, I knew a young, immature, perfectly typical couple who fell madly in love. By the end of our first semester, they announced, "We're getting married in a month!" Many of their Christian friends replied, "Why? Are you sure that's God's will?" And they confidently asserted, "We've prayed about it a lot, and we know it's God's will."

Under the traditional view of God's individual will, we were all supposed to say, "Wow, they've prayed about it and discovered that God's will for them violates common sense. How dare we attempt to warn or caution them?" By couching their choice as God's will, they communicated, "Do you have a problem with God's will? Who are you to question God? We're getting married. If you have any complaints, take them up with God." Claiming God's will is like the ace card that trumps all argument. "Well, I can't contradict God," we're supposed to say, "So I had better let you drive off a cliff."

Most sane people (particularly parents) would agree that in general, it is not a wise idea for a young couple to meet, fall in love, and get married in a three-month span. Of course there's the exception, that rare and special couple who got married after knowing each other thirteen days and just celebrated their sixtieth anniversary. To them, we can all say, "Congratulations, and let's write 'grace' all over that and be grateful!" Despite the rare exceptions, in general, a rushed marriage is not a wise plan, and God is never honored when we blame our lack of wisdom.

When others try to back us off and thus distance themselves from wise counsel or accountability with the "God's will" defense, we don't have to be silenced. We can calmly, compassionately say, "What I see in this choice is mostly your will. You're the one making the decision, and I'd like you to consider that God would never lead you to choose an action that contradicts the wisdom of His Word and His people." If a decision is truly God's will, then we cannot question it, but if we see most decisions as expressions of human will (no matter what the deciders try to call them), then we have an opportunity to approach them in love and express a biblical alternative for a potentially wiser choice. Walking in wisdom and helping others to do the same is truly the will of God according to the Word of God.

When Do I Speak Up?

The closer the relationship, the more likely God would want us to intervene. For example, even Moses, leading the people of Israel, did not intervene in the life of every person making every wrong decision every day. Nor did he allow others that kind of access to the decisions he was wrestling through. However, he did open up his life to the wise eyes of his father-in-law, Jethro, and he listened to Jethro's candid and compassionate advice: **"What you are doing is not good"** (Exod. 18:17). Out of love, Jethro pointed out that Moses was working himself into the ground and suggested a new model for delegation and sharing the burden of leadership—and Moses took that sound counsel to heart. **"So Moses listened**

to the voice of his father-in-law and did all that he had said"
(18:24), and that revolutionized Moses's life and leadership.

Just as Jethro challenged Moses, so we need to be willing
to challenge the life and relationship choices of those closest
to us. For example, do we back away from or confront a couple
who's throwing in the towel on their marriage? Let's say this
couple at one time claimed to love one another, committed
their lives to each another, started raising a family, and then
all of a sudden concluded, "Well, we've talked it through, and
we're no longer in love like we once were. We've both prayed
about it, and we want to be amicable about this. We've decided
that it's God's will for us to get a divorce." Should we back
away in silence?

Is it God's will for them to get a divorce? No, it is not.
This is not the place to explicate a full, biblical view on marriage and divorce, but we can note that except for some rare,
extreme cases, it is not God's will for people to divorce. God
makes narrow provisions for divorce, but He never mandates it.
His Word clearly tells us His high view of marriage. But when
we start contriving some personalized, customized will of God
that allows us to do what we want and then claim it is God's
will, we isolate ourselves from the family of faith that is supposed to sound the alarm when we begin to get off course and
away from God's Word. The "God's will" card may allow you
to limit the pressure of true accountability, but it doesn't lead
to sanctification or joy, which we do know *IS* God's will for us!

Blessing #5: We can avoid indecision.

The Bible gives absolutely no plan for discovering God's individual will. In fact, the idea of a personalized, divine will for our lives creates a lot of indecision. People spend inordinate amounts of time agonizing between good choices. Believers are stuck waiting for "the revelation," looking for it and longing for it while important decisions need to be made. People can become dangerously indecisive, or worse, they can manufacture evidence to prove to themselves that God has in fact directed them individually. Those who insist that faith involves waiting for God's go-ahead on every decision often end up angry at God for not being specific. They resent Him, even though God has given them a wonderful opportunity to make many small choices according to their preference and all big decisions in accord with scriptural wisdom.

For example, some sincere Christians practice what can only be described as Bible roulette. Wanting to know God's will, they flip open the pages of a Bible and drop their finger down on a verse, expecting God to direct their random pointer finger. They will take words and phrases out of context, apply them to situations they are facing, and make tragic decisions.

An old story told by preachers summarizes and captures this tragic approach. A man became depressed and wanted God to direct his life. God's Word says he needed faith and the encouragement of his brothers and sisters (Heb. 10:24–25). But he was looking for a direct word from God, so he flipped open the Bible and slammed down his finger on Matthew 27:5, **"He went and hanged himself."**

That jolted him, so he tried again, flipping the Bible pages and jabbing his finger down on Luke 10:37, where Jesus said, **"You go, and do likewise."** Those words sent a chill up his spine. Hoping for some relief, he tried a third time, landing on John 13:27, **"What you are going to do, do quickly."** Bible roulette is a foolish, dangerous way of trying to determine God's will!

So are Christian fortune cookies. Well-meaning Christians buy Scripture memory cards (sometimes shaped like loaves of bread or treasure boxes). They flip open the lid, draw the card, and expect to magically get a word from God regarding their lives. These simple tools designed for Bible memorization get misused as God's will-telling oracles. Rather than relying on the wisdom of God's open Word and the power of the Holy Spirit, they want to treat God as a fortune-teller and His holy Word like a crystal ball. He wrote a whole Book for us! And we are to study **"to present yourself to God as one approved, a worker who has no need to be ashamed, rightly handling the word of truth"** (2 Tim. 2:15).

All of this can lead to great heartache. Early in my ministry, I was told the story of a pastor who was heartbroken over a personal tragedy—battling a very serious disease, his wife was dying in the hospital. Desperate, the husband flipped open a Bible promise box and drew a card with the words of

John 11:26: **"and everyone who lives and believes in me shall never die. Do you believe this?"** The very next card offered Psalm 118:17, **"I shall not die, but I shall live, and recount the deeds of the LORD."** The pastor should have known better, but in his grief, he took those two cards to the hospital and told his wife, "You're not going to die." He appealed to the cards as proof, claiming them as a specific message from God. He confidently told the doctors and nurses, "She's not going to die." He reassured his church, "I got a special message from the Lord. God told me she's not going to die." He waved the cards as proof, but his wife died. And because of how God's Word was mishandled, reproach was brought on the name of Christ, and people began to doubt. We must carefully, wisely handle God's Word.

In addition to Bible roulette and Christian fortune cookies is the first-thought approach. An old friend of mine explained, "Whenever I want to know what God's will is, I just pull the lever on my recliner, lie back in the chair, put my feet up, and try to clear my mind of every single, possible thought. Once my mind is completely empty, the next thought that occurs to me—that's God's will for me." Perhaps that's more aptly called the "empty-headed" approach to God's will, and that is such a bad plan! It provides an invitation to Satan. Jesus gave a chilling description of what happens to an empty space that isn't immediately filled with something good (Matt. 12:43–45). The Bible never tells us to clear our minds of everything. The

Bible does tell us to fill our minds with the truth of God's Word (Rom. 12:2).

We can be drawn into silly little superstitions, trying to discover or even control God's so-called specific will for our lives. I remember a college friend who was interested in a girl but feared the possible rejection of asking her out, so he devised a plan that played out awkwardly and comically. He would reach for the phone, dial, then hang up before it connected. Finally he would announce, "If she picks up on the first ring, I'm supposed to talk to her." He would anxiously dial the number and listen as the phone rang—long past the first ring, cheating on his own little test. Finally he would slam the receiver down, half-angry that she didn't answer, half-relieved. Like him, many genuine believers can get caught up in trying to discover an individual plan for life's minutiae, only to discover the hard way that it does not exist.

Blessing #6: We can reduce subjectivity.

Subjectivity involves emotional choices, making decisions detached from any verifiable facts. Feelings and hunches rule a subjective person. In the train of life, emotions make a great caboose, but they make a lousy engine. When emotions take the lead, they can really lead you astray. If anger, euphoria, or even boredom is the primary motivation behind a decision, you should wait for a better reason. If you reflect back on the decisions in your life that you most regret, how many were emotional, spur-of-the-moment decisions? An emotional decision will gratify you for a short time but can shame you for a lifetime. Do not make emotional decisions.

Sometimes we think strong feelings are proof of God's will. Powerful emotions, such as that feeling of first falling in love, can influence us to make rash, unwise decisions. Instead of following our hearts, God expects us to use our minds and His wisdom when we make decisions, which can greatly reduce dangerous emotionalism. For more on this subject, see *Decision Making by the Book: How to Choose Wisely in an Age of Options* by Haddon Robinson, who was my professor in my doctoral studies at Denver Seminary. This excellent book addresses in detail many of the issues involved in correctly using the Bible as a guide and resource in decision-making.

In his book, Dr. Robinson tells the story of a woman who was deciding whether or not to travel to California. She was praying for God's will and glanced up at her clock, which read "7:47." Immediately she connected this to a 747 airplane and was convinced this was God's sign for her to go. Dr. Robinson recounts that he would have been more impressed if the clock had read "7:67" or "DC-10."

The fact that God knows what you will choose does *not* mean you must choose the right thing. Desperate to discover this elusive "God's will for me," people reach foolish, subjective conclusions. When this becomes a pattern, we are being led around by our emotions, and this elevation of emotions to a place of authority in our lives causes misapplication of Scripture and dangerous decision-making. A common example is the way Christians handle Colossians 3:15, which Paul included in a series of practical instructions about living with other believers in the fallen world. He wrote, **"And let the peace of Christ rule in your hearts, to which indeed you were called in one body. And be thankful."**

Since the time I was very young, I was taught that a key element in making good decisions is the question, "Do you have a sense of peace about it?" After all, as long as you feel peaceful inside, the decision must be the right one, right? Among Christians, the standard of "having peace" is primarily derived from this verse, which has nothing to do with wise decision-making.

Here's the argument: "Pastor James, I've really studied Colossians 3:15. The word *rule* means direct or act as an umpire, so the verse means that we must let God's peace act as an umpire. What I've discovered is that when I'm out of God's will, I feel anxiety and discomfort, which feels an awful lot like an umpire's whistle. But when I'm in God's will, I feel peace, which is the Holy Spirit's confirmation that I'm doing God's will. As long as I have that sense of peace, I know I'm in God's will for me."

But let's go back to Scripture and check the context of this verse. This entire chapter is all about living as a person who has been **"raised with Christ"** (3:1). It includes a series of broad commands that give us reliable direction:

"Seek the things that are above" (3:1).

"Set your minds on things that are above" (3:2).

"Put to death therefore what is earthly in you" (3:5).

"Put on then, as God's chosen ones, holy and beloved, compassionate hearts, kindness, humility, meekness, and patience" (3:12).

"Put on love" (3:14).

"And let the peace of Christ rule in your hearts" (3:15).

"And be thankful" (3:15).

"Let the word of Christ dwell in you richly" (3:16).

"Do everything in the name of the Lord Jesus" (3:17).

That "peace priority" looks a little different among the active commands that surround it. How often do we miss opportunities to put all the other commands on this list into practice while we passively "wait for peace"? The last four items on the list above are results that follow practicing the first five commands. And we cannot miss the tone of this entire passage. The context is relational strife. The heart of this chapter isn't verse 15 but verses 12 and 13. Read them slowly: **"Put on then, as God's chosen ones, holy and beloved, compassionate hearts, kindness, humility, meekness, and patience, bearing with one another and, if one has a complaint against another, forgiving each other; as the Lord has forgiven you, so you also must forgive"** (Col. 3:12–13).

What happens when an emotional argument erupts between you and me? Relational strife rears its ugly head. According to Colossians 3, I'm supposed to wrap myself in compassion, kindness, humility, meekness, and patience. Practicing those godly traits does serious damage to personal offenses like stung pride and bitterness. Then I must reach out to bear with you, because in developing the character traits above I gain a new appreciation for how much you have to bear with me. Out of these discoveries, I must forgive, remembering that love is the first and last thing people ought to experience among Christians. When I've taken care of all this, then I'm supposed to let the peace of Christ rule in my heart. So if I have some anxiety or tension in my heart, I need to get to you quickly and work out the fault between us in our relationship so that I can have peace again. The peace of Christ is the awareness that I have done my part, out of obedience to Christ, to remove relational strife. Among believers, that leads to good feelings, including peace.

According to God's Word, we must forgive, we must love, and we must work toward relational peace with all people. Romans 12:18 drives home this point: **"If possible, so far as it depends on you, live peaceably with all."** That's the point of Colossians 3:15. It has absolutely nothing to do with a peaceful sense of finality in a decision about something uncertain as a signal for me that God agrees and everything to do with forging relational peace.

So let's declare a moratorium on asking people if they have peace about their decisions. Hard, truthful, God-honoring decisions often come with feelings like fear, discomfort, and even pain. Meanwhile, countless willfully sinful actions are taken by people who report feeling at peace about their choices.

> Let's declare a moratorium on asking people if they have peace about their decisions.

Take Jonah, for example. The prophet coldly, calmly, and deliberately ran away from God's direct orders. The ship he boarded for his escape sailed into a nightmare of a storm. While the crew was fighting for their lives, Jonah was hunkered below deck, snug and fast asleep. Jonah was feeling the peace of an apparently successful escape from his role in God's sovereign will. During the storm, was Jonah in God's will? No, he was not, but he sure felt peace. Was God's sovereign will thwarted by Jonah's detour? No. God continued to shape events to follow His master plan: the rescue of the lost souls of Ninevah. Consider the end of Jonah's story, when he finally was following God's will. Did he feel a sense of peace then? No! He was grumpy and angry, still chafing at God's compassion. Jonah's story illustrates that peaceful feelings are not a dependable measure of obedience or God's will.

If that challenges our traditional thinking, we can also study Jesus in the Garden of Gethsemane. Was Jesus following God's will? Perfectly, always. **"Not my will, but yours, be done,"** Jesus prayed (Luke 22:42). Did Jesus feel a sense of peace? No! In fact, the tension of obedience to God was so great that Jesus sweat **"great drops of blood"** (22:44). Peace is not primarily about feelings but about the cooperation of truth and action. Jesus never lost the state of peace with God because He willingly accepted feelings that were anything but peaceful. Let's dispense with the notion that obedience to God always brings good feelings and that disobedience brings anxiety.

Peaceful feelings are simply not a reliable indicator of wise decision-making. Relying on peaceful feelings can lead to awful decisions. By recognizing that God's will *IS* that we apply His wisdom and guidance to our decision-making, we reduce the subjectivity of our choices.

> Peaceful feelings are simply not a reliable indicator of wise decision-making.

Those are six of the blessings that flow from conforming our beliefs to Scripture. God's Word leads us to set aside the notion that we are seeking a personalized, customized will of God for our lives. We replace that doomed quest with obedience to God's Word in our decision-making. We decide to place the weight of most of our choices on what God has already said, rather than on vague hopes that He might have some individu-alized, personalized direction for us. This results in the follow-ing evidences of a healthy spiritual life:

- freedom from anxiety and guilt
- freedom to recognize the validity of equal options
- freedom to challenge immature and unwise decisions of loved ones—and an openness to having our own decisions challenged
- freedom from indecision
- confident choices with minimal subjectivity

In the next chapter, we will explore how to make everyday, wise choices that please God. He cares deeply about you and the choices you make—but He has not chosen to make most of them for you. There's no secret, detailed, hidden plan that you are supposed to be decoding. As long as you are roaming the lush green pastures of God's Word, He is pleased and you are doing what His will *IS* when you seek to make wise decisions.

Father God,

I am confident in Your ability to accomplish Your sovereign will. Nothing will undermine Your master plan. I commit myself to obeying Your Word. Thank You for those instructions for living. So I accept that I need not worry about a hidden plan for my life. Please help me to make wise decisions, to be committed to Your Word, to be open to hearing from Your people, and to trust that You can handle whatever I choose. Thank You for the challenge and freedom to serve You. In the name of Jesus, my Savior and Master, I pray. Amen.

CHAPTER 5

A Wonderful Freedom

THE DEMOLITION IS complete.

In the first few chapters, we razed some traditional, dearly held, but unbiblical assumptions about the individualized will of God. We have cleared the site of false ideals and are ready to start building a new understanding of God's will.

Assuming you have read this far in the book (and didn't just flip to chapter 5), then I can likely conclude that you want to both *know* and *do* God's will. If either of those desires is missing, that indicates a serious spiritual problem. Assuming both desires are alive in you, you are ready to read on.

So far, we have done the easy part of the process. Pointing out what is wrong is simpler than offering a practical alternative. When an idea has been enshrined as tradition, seeing it in a new, biblical light can feel unnerving. In chapters 2 and 3, we challenged the traditional view of God's individual will, the idea that God has a detailed, specific, individual blueprint for each of His children's lives, which if not decoded precisely, leads to grave consequences. In chapter 4, we went after particular verses of Scripture used to defend the traditional view of God's will and offered what I hope is a better and more contextual understanding of those verses. At this point, I hope we have successfully demolished the old structure and cleared the way for the exciting adventure of following what the will of God *IS*.

Other Contractors

Fear not, I did not dream up this perspective on God's will while sitting alone in my office. I am not the lone voice crying in the wilderness. In fact, I'm in excellent company. Most people who have given their lives to carefully studying God's Word conclude that God doesn't fit the role of micromanager. A biblical understanding of God's will is good news for those who have been living lives of quiet desperation because they are convinced they have lost sight of God's will or God has lost sight of them!

Many Christians hear this as new teaching. It isn't. The idea of an individualized will of God is actually not that traditional in the scope of Christian history. Only for the past 150 years or so has it become the popular understanding of God's Word. We are not inventing new turf; we're rediscovering the biblical turf occupied by the church for most of the past two thousand years.

Ultimately, I want you to live in freedom because it is true, not because you read or heard it from me. I want you to see how it is rooted in Scripture, and I want you to see the truth confirmed by others who are also deeply committed to teaching God's Word. Let me introduce you to a few.

At a time in my life when all I could see were the problems in the so-called individual will of God, I read a book that has become a modern classic on the topic. *Decision Making and the Will of God*, by Garry Friesen, has become the benchmark for those who want to think deeply about all the biblical teaching surrounding the will of God. If you read it, the degree to which Garry has influenced me will be obvious. When that book was released, Garry really was like a voice crying in the wilderness, pointing people back to the Word of God as a foundation for understanding God's will. Here is one of my favorite challenges from Friesen:

> It is commonly taught that for each person, God has an *individual will*—an ideal, detailed life-plan for each person. In this traditional view, the key to decision-making is to discover God's individual will, and then do it. Accordingly, the burden of most books on guidance is to explain how to discern God's specific leading in each situation. By contrast, the emphasis of Scripture is on God's moral will. In fact, the Bible

reveals nothing of an "individual will" governing each decision.[3]

Another voice that often echoes in my mind is John MacArthur's, who is such a well-known and loved Bible teacher. He wrote a practical little book called *Found: God's Will*. MacArthur has a unique and powerful way of stating his case:

> You see, the will of God is not primarily a place. The will of God is not, first of all, for you to go there or work here. The will of God concerns you as a person. If you are the right you, you can follow your desires and you will fulfill God's will.[4]

Returning to Haddon Robinson and his powerful book, *Decision Making by the Book*, we are confronted with a healthy challenge:

> We are shocked when we turn to the Bible and discover that asking the question: "How do we know the will of God for life's tough decisions?" isn't a biblical question! God does not encourage us to ask the question and even more significantly, God gives us no answer. The Bible's silence almost shouts at us.[5]

Among respected Bible teachers, there is broad-based agreement on the teaching in this book. It is not unusual; it is biblical. And it's what Christians actually believed about God's will for most of church history. God's will is not about where you live, what you buy, or what you drive. God's will *IS* about the kind of person you are becoming.

These are just a few of the fellow contractors whom I'm privileged to work alongside in building a firm foundation for you upon the solid rock of God's Word.

Digging the Footings

Whenever I find resistance to clear biblical teaching, I know I'm messing with hidden (and often cherished) beliefs that are incorrect. Three items of "spiritual debris" need to be cleared from our spiritual construction site in order to finish this foundation. Let's consider the three, primary reasons we unconsciously or deliberately resist the biblical teaching on God's will. We resist the biblical teaching on God's will for several reasons:

Reason 1: We tend to treat biblical characters as normative.

It's one thing to say, "If God did this for them, then He *could* do it for me." It's something else entirely to say, "God did this for them, so He *must* do the same for me."

The characters whose lives and experiences are recorded in the Bible were often led by God in what appear to us to be obvious, easy-to-obey ways. But we can't overlook the fact that it is because their stories are unique that they are recorded in God's Word. We must also remember that much of what we know now as God's Word was not available to the characters in Scripture. We have the written Word of God, and precisely because they did not, they more often heard from God in other ways. The writer of Hebrews reminds us of this crucial difference at the beginning of his letter: **"Long ago, at many times and in many ways, God spoke to our fathers by the prophets, but in these last days he has spoken to us by his Son, whom he appointed the heir of all things, through whom also he created the world"** (Heb. 1:1–2).

Does this mean we can't learn from the stories of the people in the Bible? Of course not! Paul tells us in 1 Corinthians 10:11, **"Now these things happened to them as an example, but they were written down for our instruction, on whom the end of the ages has come."** We can certainly find examples among Bible people and receive instruction from their experiences, but we go too far if we try to make their lives a template for our own. Our Shepherd doesn't treat each of us alike. He knows exactly what each of us needs.

Consider the life of Moses. A too-literal reader might peruse Exodus 3 and decide, *I am going to stand beside a bush in the backyard, and when God lights it on fire, then I'll know He's trying to tell me something.* That confused reader has skipped over most of the lessons in the biblical account and rushed right to a point the story doesn't make. The most obvious problem with this "personal application" is that it is based on a faulty mental picture of the event rather than the description of

Moses's experience. Moses was not standing expectantly beside a bush, waiting for God to speak to him. At first, Moses didn't even realize that the burning bush had something to do with God. He wasn't looking for God's will; he was just curious about that odd bush. Moses didn't realize that God had been taking him through an eighty-year training exercise to prepare him to lead the chosen people out of Egypt. Moses didn't know God had scheduled a graduation and commissioning service for him out in the desert. The burning bush for Moses was like the whale that swallowed Jonah—divinely appointed but totally unexpected. According to Exodus 2:11–15, Moses had tried to exercise leadership forty years before in Egypt and had failed miserably. God took drastic measures to accomplish His purposes: "Here comes Moses; fire up the bush!"

> The burning bush for Moses was like the whale that swallowed Jonah—divinely appointed but totally unexpected.

Is this story true? Yes.

Was there a real, burning bush that was not consumed by the flames? Yes.

Did God's voice speak to Moses from the flames? Yes.

But should we expect God to issue His directions to us through flaming shrubbery? No!

God has managed the universe for a long time and accomplished His purposes through the lives of many faithful (and not-so-faithful) people, and He has only used a burning bush once. What do you think the odds are that He's going to decide to use one with you?

Why do we resist the biblical teaching on God's will?

Reason 2: The biblical teaching on God's will conflicts with our priorities.

Let's be honest: What often matters most to us is our own lives. Becoming the people God wants us to be is relegated to the back burner. Too often we want God to get excited about our dreams and plans, confirming for us the car/house/person/ job that makes us feel complete. But as we grow and mature in our faith, we learn that life isn't about God's getting on our program; it's about our getting on God's program. The individualized view of God's will makes God's purposes more about me than about God. But the biblical teaching on God's will tramples all over our little plans and schemes. Our instinct is to alter the teaching rather than alter our view. How often we claim to be trying to find God's will, but really we are trying to get our own way. We forget that God's ultimate purpose in messing with our plans is to give us something much better! This is the second reason why we may have accepted a warped understanding of God's will.

> Life isn't about God's getting on our program; it's about our getting on God's program.

A sobering and extreme example of this distortion can be found in the account of Ananias and Sapphira in Acts 5:1–11. As the early church grew and persecution intensified in Jerusalem, the believers willingly shared with each other in order to survive. Many sold property to provide funds for the group. Was it God's will that they generously help each other? Yes. Was it God's will that everyone sell everything? No. Yet after Ananias and Sapphira sold their land, they kept part of the money for themselves but lied about it. Peter confronted them. **"But Peter said, 'Ananias, why has Satan filled your heart to lie to the Holy Spirit and to keep back for yourself part of the proceeds of the land? While it remained unsold, did it not remain your own? And after it was sold, was it not at your disposal? Why is it that you have contrived this deed in your heart? You have not lied to man but to God'"** (Acts 5:3–4).

The sin of Ananias and Sapphira was their desire to appear generous while practicing greed. They wanted to look the part of participating in God's will, loving their neighbors and meeting their needs, while in reality they were watching out only for themselves. They tragically twisted God's will into just a pretense of generosity. It is always dangerous for us to proclaim with our mouths that we are doing God's will when our hearts and actions show we are only interested in doing our own. Time to end the charade of appearing to be in God's will and do the hard work of what God's will truly *IS*.

Why do we resist the biblical teaching on God's will?

Reason 3: The biblical teaching on God's will doesn't square with our understanding of control.

God is in control of all things. The Bible proclaims and abundantly illustrates this divine sovereignty. But we take these powerful truths and subject them to a human perspective on the meaning of control. "If God is *ultimately* in control of all things," we may reason, "then He must be *intimately* in control of all things. He must have a will for every detail."

That line of thinking is not supported by the Bible, by reason, or by experience. Here's the cool thing about God. He doesn't have to control everything to control everything. God is not like us. If we were in charge, we would have to micromanage everything; that's the only way we can imagine being in control of everything. But God doesn't have our limitations.

Consider the logic. If we argued that God controls every, single, little detail of every life, the idea of making choices stops making sense, yet God's Word treats our decision-making seriously. What we choose matters. How far it matters (whether it affects things on a large scale) is up to God, but our decisions certainly matter in our lives and in the lives of those connected to us. And the fact remains: God can control everything without controlling everything.

God doesn't have to dictate every minute detail to make sure His will is accomplished. He's that awesome! He leaves some freedom to us in the details we choose. We might be tempted to think, *Well, if I hadn't moved onto that street, I wouldn't have had an opportunity to share Christ with my neighbor, and he wouldn't have gotten saved. My neighbor's eternal destiny rested on my decision to choose that particular house.* That is simply untrue. God overrules. If we didn't arrive on the scene for that neighbor, God

> God can control everything without controlling everything.

is perfectly capable of getting the gospel to him or her another way. We need to be responsible to the neighbors we actually have, not the ones we might have had if we had moved somewhere else.

God is not limited by the choices we make, which is why He gives us freedom within the boundaries of His Word. Ephesians 1:11 describes our God **"who works all things according to the counsel of his will,"** which means that God ultimately decides the outcome of all things. The same God who had the first word when He created will also have the last word about the creation as we know it. He will not allow anything to happen that would hinder the accomplishment of His purposes—which is crazy to say because *nothing* could *ever* hinder His purposes.

We explored three reasons why we resist the biblical teaching on God's will:

Reason 1: We tend to treat biblical characters as normative.

Reason 2: The biblical teaching on God's will conflicts with our priorities.

Reason 3: The biblical teaching on God's will doesn't square with our understanding of control.

If we have truly laid those reasons to rest, clearing them from our spiritual foundation, then we are ready to lay a new foundation for our everyday experience of following God's will. Ready?

God's Will: Layer 1

What is God's will for your life? *The first layer of a proper foundation is submission to God's sovereign will.* God's will is for us to submit to His sovereign will, because it deals with matters over which we have no control. We function best when we are consciously dependent on God for our very existence. We never translate our responsibility into independence from God. This shapes the way we make plans. One of the practical connections between God's sovereign will and our capacity for planning can be found in James 4:13–15: **"Come now, you who say, 'Today or tomorrow we will go into such and such a town and spend a year there and trade and make a profit'— yet you do not know what tomorrow will bring. What is your life? For you are a mist that appears for a little time and then**

vanishes. Instead you ought to say, 'If the Lord wills, we will live and do this or that.'"

"If the Lord wills." Sometimes this passage is used to teach the traditional view of God's will. But is James really saying that the only wise decisions are those that perfectly match a pre-selected sequence chosen by God? Was James teaching against the wisdom of planning? No. Verse 13 identifies James's audience: those who are making plans, people who like to prepare for what's coming. They keep everything on their calendars, with handy alerts and recurring events to streamline their planning. Oh, the planners—they know who they are!

James's point is not that it's wrong to make plans. His point is that in making plans, we must keep in mind that we don't even know if we will have tomorrow. Taking tomorrow for granted is an arrogant view of the future. None of us can guarantee tomorrow. What we can recognize is that whatever happens tomorrow, God will still be in charge. So we plan, but we plan with a sober understanding of the future. We plan with the wise caveat, **"If the Lord wills."**

The lesson isn't that God has a will about **"this or that."** The point is, **"If the Lord wills, we will live"** (James 4:15). It's an injunction against the presumption of thinking that we're in control of the length of our lives. Obviously we aren't. We don't know how much time we have.

One of the problems with the micromanagement view of God's will is it puts our lives on hold. It causes us to alter our reading of this verse and conclude, "*When* the Lord wills, we will live and do this or that." It puts our knowing God's will ahead of making a decision. It puts planning and deciding on hold until we know God's will. It turns us into parked vehicles waiting for steering directions, rather than vehicles in motion, doing what we already know of God's will from His Word and expecting Him to steer when necessary. We acknowledge our need for steering and God's sovereign ability to steer even while we are in motion. A parked vehicle doesn't need steering, and it's difficult to plan when you are stuck in park!

Is it okay for us to make plans for the future? What did Jesus say? **"So don't worry about tomorrow, for tomorrow will bring its own worries. Today's trouble is enough for today"** (Matt. 6:34 NLT). Now some who hold the common view of God's will twist this verse to make a case against planning. Was Jesus telling us not to plan? No, He was telling us not to worry about tomorrow. For most people, one of the effective ways to handle our bent toward anxiety is to make some God-honoring plans. In other words, *lack of planning* is often an underlying cause for persistent worry! God gave us the ability to think ahead for a reason—so we can plan. We can practice worry-free living by framing our plans with James's pattern: **"If the Lord wills, we will live and do this or that"** (James 4:15). This approach allows us to look at the future wisely and confidently—knowing we've done our best and trusting that God has things under control.

By consciously recognizing God's sovereignty, we avoid presumption. Then we don't falsely assume we are in control of anything, even the freedom we have to make choices about **"this or that."** We exercise our freedom to make plans: "Next Thursday we have scheduled a family night out," or "We're going on vacation in October," or even, "My goal is to accomplish these three items in my business before Labor Day." But we never forget that the freedom we have to make those choices is given to us by a sovereign God.

As if to drive home his point, James adds a warning: **"As it is, you boast in your arrogance. All such boasting is evil"** (James 4:16). What boasting is evil? The boasting of making and announcing plans without considering God's sovereign right to overrule any scheme or strategy we devise. Instead, our plans can be made humbly, acknowledging that God's will is for us to submit to His sovereign will.

Uncontrollables

Even though we can make wise plans, there is so much in life outside our control. What are some of the things in life we cannot control? When are we most likely to face situations where we must be submissive to God's sovereign will?

Our health is in God's hands. We can control a sliver of our health: healthy eating habits, exercise, regular doctor visits, adequate rest. Yet regardless of how rigid our diets or how many sit-ups we do, we can't alter our genetic make-up. People in great shape die every day. James's words take on fresh meaning: **"If the Lord wills, we will live"** (James 4:15)—literally!

The weather reminds us of how little control we have. Because of advanced weather tracking, we can prepare for certain weather events, like hurricanes, but we can't change them. Powerful winds and waves can make toothpicks out of architects' masterpieces. Other weather events take us completely by surprise, such as earthquakes. No matter how much we prepare for storms, heed warnings, and retreat from natural disasters, the weather reminds us how fragile human life is and how much we depend on God for whether or not we live tomorrow.

Our finances can feel like a natural disaster too. Some aspects of money management are within our control, such as our discretionary spending or hard work ethic. Some, like an earthquake, are completely out of our hands, such as a market crash, job loss, or crippling medical bill. The more we practice good stewardship, the more aware we become that matters are often beyond our ability to prepare for or predict. The best budget doesn't guarantee financial security. Ignoring God's sovereignty doesn't make these possibilities disappear; it simply makes them even more devastating. Conversely, acknowledging God's sovereignty doesn't prevent hardships from happening, but it gives us Someone to turn to when trouble comes.

While we have a measure of control over our own choices, we cannot control other people's decisions and actions, which may have a ripple effect upon those we love most. We don't have to look any further than our own children to realize that. Our kids have ways of saying and doing things that make us feel helpless. Those little babies that relied completely on us grow up all too quickly into young people who often insist on exercising their independence and learning things the hard way.

Any personal illusions we may have about the degree of human control in life are exploded by the calls that come into a church office. Heart-rending medical reports, from babies born in distress to the unexpected twists cancer brings to middle age to the painful stages at the end of life. Sudden, devastating tragedies, from car accidents to job losses to abuse and abandonment. Each call is a reminder that there is a sovereign God who controls the universe and has appointed to each of us a season of adversity, over which we have zero control. And God's will *IS* that we would submit to Him in matters that we cannot control.

Submitting to God's sovereign will touches a raw nerve in many people. They wonder if submission requires a passive approach to life's issues. They want to know what submission to God looks like in the middle of life's impossible, nearly unbearable situations. "How do I put submission into action?" they ask.

Submission to God *sounds* like something we can describe, even if we can't describe what submission *feels* like. Submission causes us to say, "I trust You, Lord. No matter what, I trust You." This phrase should be constantly on the mind, heart, and lips of every follower of Jesus. When difficult times come, before we even take time to figure out a reason, we respond with an expression of trust. We don't have to know why something happened in order to continue trusting God. We can say, "Lord, I'm going to trust You in this. I believe You are good; I believe You are faithful. Even if I can't see Your goodness right now, I want to, so I will wait for You to show me."

> We don't have to know why something happened in order to continue trusting God.

The waiting can take a while. God is not on our timetable. But the longer I live, the more I anticipate the amazing scene when we get to heaven, when everything will suddenly be clear. We will understand. Life will make sense in God's glorious, awesome presence. We will see God's overarching, sovereign plan. The divine wisdom of God's actions will then be obvious. And even though we can't see that now, one day we will be able to look back and say, "Although I couldn't see it all,

I trusted God and kept following Him. It was hard sometimes, but God is faithful." We can trust in God's sovereign will.

God's Will: Layer 2

What is God's will for your life? *The second layer of a proper foundation is knowing that God wants us to be sanctified by His Word.* God has delivered the bulk of His will to us in the form of the Bible. Whenever we talk about knowing and obeying God's will, we are primarily talking about what God has spelled out in His Word. If you want to know God's will regarding your behavior, conduct, and actions—look for clear answers in the Bible. Back to the parked car analogy, a believer's life should never be in park, sitting still, waiting to know God's will. There is always plenty of God's Word to put into practice.

To be sanctified by God's Word means that we are being shaped and trained by God's directions toward Christlikeness. God not only tells us what He wants us to do, but He also tells us why: **"Finally, then, brothers, we ask and urge you in the Lord Jesus, that as you received from us how you ought to walk and to please God, just as you are doing, that you do so more and more"** (1 Thess. 4:1).

In our conduct and choices, God's will is that we would please Him. How does the idea that you can please God with your life strike you as an answer to your desire to know God's will? Even your desire to want to please God is pleasing to God.

No matter what time of the day you are reading this, you have probably already made numerous choices, large and small, since you woke up this morning. You likely didn't stop before making each choice to consider whether that choice was God's will. If you had, you might still be paralyzed in front of your coffee-maker. But what would it be like to live each day with the overarching desire to please God? Instead of trying to make every single, little choice conform to some predetermined, straitjacket will of God, you can seek to please Him, knowing that as you follow His Word, He's sanctifying you in the process. Just because God doesn't have an individual will for your life doesn't mean He doesn't know and care deeply about the choices you make. He does! Your choices can please Him and also grieve Him.

> Even your desire to want to please God is pleasing to God.

And pleasing Him leads to His glory and our good. The apostle Paul continues, **"For you know what instructions we gave you through the Lord Jesus. For this is the will of God, your sanctification: that you abstain from sexual immorality"** (1 Thess. 4:2–3).

What word jumps out at you in those verses? *Sanctification.* That may not be a word we use in everyday conversation, but it should define our everyday lives. It's one of the most important words in the Christian life. After "cross," "conversion," and "salvation," "sanctification" covers the rest of life on this side of eternity. Sanctification is the lifelong process of being set apart, being made righteous, becoming more Christlike. The word captures the work God begins in our lives starting at the moment of salvation and continuing through our last breath. **"And I am sure of this,"** Paul writes, **"that he who began a good work in you will bring it to completion at the day of Jesus Christ"** (Phil. 1:6).

The process of being set apart gets personal and practical right away. Notice the last phrase in 1 Thessalonians 4:3: **"that you abstain from sexual immorality."** The Bible has a high view of sex and a low view of sexual immorality. God's Word builds a wall of protection around a wonderful gift from God. When God asks us to abstain from anything, He has good reasons, and the results are always for our good. The result of staying within God's Word on sex is **"that each one of you know how to control his own body in holiness and honor, not in the passion of lust like the Gentiles who do not know God"** (1 Thess. 4:4–5).

God wants us to live like people who know Him! What do we want? I sure don't want to live like a person who doesn't know Him. I don't want to live for myself, giving into temptation and selfish desires, like those who don't know God. I want to live with a healthy sense of self-control that brings holiness and honor to my life. I don't want to live on a destructive roller coaster of ever-changing passions. And I don't want to be a person who merely says he knows God; I want to be a person who lives like he knows God, seeking to please Him.

> It is God's sovereign will that we be sanctified by His Word, which always involves the way we know Him and the way we treat one another.

Sanctification encompasses the vertical aspect of our intimacy with God, and it also covers our horizontal relationships with others. In Paul's words, **"that no one transgress and wrong his brother in this matter, because the Lord is an avenger in all these things, as we told you beforehand and solemnly warned you. For God has not called us for impurity, but in holiness. Therefore whoever disregards this, disregards not man but God, who gives his Holy Spirit to you"** (1 Thess. 4:6–9). It is God's sovereign will that we be sanctified by His Word, which always involves the way we know Him and the way we treat one another.

Notice how the Bible describes God's will for our lives. The focus is never on externals: where, when, with whom; that's our focus. We ask,

- Where should I live?
- Where should I work?

- Where should I go to school?
- Whom should I marry?
- Whom should I befriend?
- Whom should I reach out to?

God focuses on

- Is this the decision of a Christ-follower?
- How does this action reveal My Son?
- Is this consistent with My Word?
- Why do you want to do this?
- How does this show My heart?

When we are concerned with doing God's will, we will shift our focus to God's set of questions.

Sanctification isn't our project, as if just trying harder will make us Christlike. Consider Paul's understated reminder of our constant Companion on this journey of sanctification: the Holy Spirit (1 Thess. 4:8). Through the Holy Spirit, God actively makes Himself known to us, increasing our sensitivity to His ways as He guides us through His Word.

I'll never forget a chapel speaker I heard in college. I was training to serve the Lord, consumed at the time with seeking the dot of God's specific will for my life. Although I can't recall his exact words, this was his message: 95 percent of God's will for you is the kind of person you are. God cares about the conversation you have at the dry cleaner—not which dry cleaner you use. God cares about the way that you drive your car—not as much which car you drive. God cares about the choices you make with your finances—and that's not a matter of finding the right vs. wrong choice; it's a matter of using wisdom.

Until that moment, I confess that for me, knowing God was mostly about *where* and *what* I would be for Him. From that moment, my attention began to shift to *who* I would be for Him, whatever I was doing or whenever I was doing it.

God's Will: Layer 3

What is God's will for your life? *The third layer of a proper foundation is being guided by His Word in matters of personal choice.* If I had to identify a central passage in Scripture that points to wise living, I would choose the following verses from Ephesians: **"Look carefully then how you walk, not as unwise but as wise, making the best use of the time, because the days are evil. Therefore do not be foolish, but understand what the will of the Lord *IS*"** (Eph. 5:15–17, emphasis mine).

In this context, the word *walk* is a euphemism for progress through life. Ephesians uses this word over and over: **"walk in a manner worthy"** (4:1), **"walk in love"** (5:2), **"walk as children of light"** (5:8). We can substitute the word *live* for *walk*, and the verses make perfect sense. But "walking" captures the continual motion of how we experience each day. The old King

James Version instructs us to **"walk circumspectly"** (5:15), meaning to walk with our eyes, looking around as we move, going through life attentively. Proverbs 4:26 says, **"Ponder the path of thy feet"** (KJV)—in other words, watch where you step!

God wants us to live wisely. For example, those who walk wisely use their time well. They are **"redeeming the time"** (Eph. 5:16 KJV), seizing the day for good choices because life is short and eternity is long. This is not just busyness. Wise people don't live at a frantic pace. They schedule rest into their lives. They don't measure a day merely by how much work gets done. They honor the fourth commandment (All ten of which are God's will summarized into ten bullet points.) by setting aside one day out of seven for a change of pace. They know that sometimes rest is the best use of time.

In contrast is the fool, who walks through life inattentively. Fools don't weigh their choices but decide on a whim. They wander through life thinking, *Well, I think I'll go over here. No, now this other thing is interesting to me, but that third thing is what I want to do with my life!* A fool has no discernment or discernible course in life. Controlled by momentary feelings, a fool fails to realize that some decisions lead to happiness, joy, and peace while other decisions lead to heartbreak, misery, and devastation.

A fool habitually and sometimes deliberately ignores the rules of life. Such a person drives over a cliff and is surprised and even resentful about the results. If you look around, you will realize that we are swimming in a sea of foolishness. Meanwhile, God's Word consistently teaches us that God's will is for us to be wise. While foolishness ignores or misuses knowledge, wisdom is the right application of knowledge. The ancient Greeks were knowledge collectors rather than knowledge appliers (see Acts 17:21). In contrast, we should **"be doers of the word, and not hearers only"** (James 1:22). The greatest fool is the person who knows better yet still chooses the wrong, unwise course of action.

Wisdom isn't about how much you know; it's about what you do with what you know. Since followers of Jesus have God's will expressed in His Word, we have a lot to inform our actions. Because we have the Bible, we have the basis for good decisions. As we learn to confidently apply the Word of God, we will make wise decisions and recognize we are traveling within the boundaries of God's will.

> If you are increasingly the kind of person God has called you to be, then you can be confident you are doing God's will.

Ephesians 5:17 captures the theme of wise living: **"Therefore do not be foolish, but understand what the will of the Lord *IS*"** (emphasis mine). Resist the thought that God's will is some ridiculous, personalized, specific list you have to find and follow exactly. God hasn't issued a painstaking prescription or blueprint for your life. These figments do not exist. Instead, God's will *IS* for you to be a certain kind of person, and if you are increasingly the kind of person God has called you to be, then you can be confident you are doing God's will.

Making Decisions

After reading this chapter, you may conclude, "Okay, I get it! God's will is about who I am in relation to Him. But I still have to figure out exactly what I'm supposed to do! How do I make good choices?"

Fair question. Once you acknowledge God's sovereignty and commit to obeying His Word, God will be able to roll with the punches of your day-to-day decisions. He will use you wherever you are. If you bloom where you are planted, God will use you. Think of Joseph, who started off with such great dreams of how God was going to use his life, until he was beaten by his brothers and sold as a slave into Egypt. Even there he tried to be faithful to God, and it landed him in a prison cell, fearing for his life. Instead of myopically scouring his résumé of suffering for where he went wrong, he believed that God's sovereign will was unfolding for his life. Confident of that, he chose to be a blessing to those around him in his place of hardship. And because he "bloomed where he was planted," that prison cell became the crucible of his sanctification. It became the launching pad for the fulfillment of the dreams God had given him so many years earlier.

If you flourish where you are, God will use you, and when He needs more of what you're doing, He'll send for you. Think of Esther, a beautiful, savvy girl in a volatile court setting, handpicked among hundreds of young women for the king's attention. Rather than wallow in the insecurity of being an orphan, of being a pawn in a royal power scheme, she faithfully made the best choices she could, and through God's sovereign will, He placed her in a position to courageously and memorably save His people.

If you focus on becoming the man or woman He's called you to be, guided by His Word in matters of personal choice to make wise decisions, then God will guide you and lead you into amazing pathways of fruitfulness and abundance in your life.

Sovereign God,

My life is in Your hands. You know me, love me, and guide me. I want to be more diligent in knowing You, loving You, and following You. Thank You for the wisdom to make good choices. I want to please You, Lord, and to become the person You have called me to be. Please continue Your sanctifying work in me through Your Holy Spirit, making me more like Your Son, Jesus Christ, my Savior and Lord. Amen.

CHAPTER 6

A Serious Accountability

WELCOME TO THE gray areas.

How should we handle situations that require personal choice? How do we make wise decisions in matters God does not prescribe through His sovereign will or His Word, topics on which the Bible does not give explicit instruction? Some of these are gray areas, some are selections between equally good outcomes, and some are simply such a part of common life that they don't feel like direct choices. God gives us freedom in those decisions. The choices are real, and we get to make them!

Survey Says

In preparation for this study, my staff surveyed one hundred people on their answers to the following survey: "Name an important life choice that God has left up to you." We compiled the top ten answers.

10. Free time
 9. Vacation
 8. Friends
 7. How to use spiritual gifts
 6. Social media and entertainment
 5. Church
 4. Spending money
 3. Car
 2. Employer
 1. Marriage partner

The most significant thing I noticed on this list was that those who were surveyed, who had been participating in an extended teaching series on God's will, demonstrated they were beginning to recognize the implications of what Scripture teaches. There are a number of decisions God expects us to own. In each category on this list (and many more), we have the responsibility to use wisdom and to seek to please God with our choices. Often the specific choice is left up to us. God offers us guidance in His Word but is most

> There are a number of decisions God expects us to own.

glorified when we use the given wisdom and make the decision ourselves.

For example, for survey answer #8, we can teach our children how to choose their friends. We shouldn't simply stumble onto our friends; we should intentionally cultivate life-giving friendships. Friendships should not be accidents but intentional choices to develop relationships with people we enjoy, who are good for us, and whose character we admire.

The choice that received the most votes—marriage partner—has certainly sparked interesting conversations. As we noted in chapter 3, some Christians have fallen into the habit of spiritualizing a romantic ideal. Our society promotes this notion that people should be scanning the globe in search of that one mystical person who perfectly suits their needs. Even people who have no interest in God talk about finding a "match made in heaven" or their "soul mate." The problem is that people wrestling this through gravitate to a feelings-based, subjective decision that may set the stage for real disappointment. What felt in the fog of romance like the perfect match seems like something else in the sunlight of practical living. And the real tragedy is that relationships with good potential are injured and sometimes destroyed by unrealistic expectations of perfection. Sadly, many people demand a level of perfection from their mate that they would never expect of themselves.

The "God's got the perfect mate for me" syndrome suggests instant, effortless, relational bliss. Instead, great marriages are lifelong construction projects. The hardest work in marriage is not the impossibility of changing my mate but the real task of changing myself. Even among believers, many people shape their lives around the objective of finding a perfect companion, yet seldom, if ever, do they ask themselves the hard question, "What does God want to do in my life that would make me an acceptable marriage partner for someone else?" Only the perfect should expect to find someone perfect!

The myth of the perfect mate is alluring but false. One biblical couple that's often dragged into the discussion is Ruth and Boaz. Talk about a great plot for a romance novel! An Israelite couple (Naomi and Elimelech) raise two strapping boys (Mahlon and Chilion) in Bethlehem during a time of famine. Eventually, they decide to relocate to Moab to escape the famine, and there Elimelech dies. In that single-parent household, each boy eventually marries a local girl. Orpah and Ruth join the family. In the following decade, tragedy strikes twice, as both sons die, leaving three women to fend for themselves. Naomi decides to return to Israel, where she hopes to find some care from extended family as a widow, so she releases her two daughters-in-law from any further commitment to her. Orpah leaves her; Ruth stays with her. Naomi and Ruth return to Bethlehem, where the lives of Boaz (a distant relative of Elimelech) and Ruth intersect. Their careful and thoughtful courtship is worth reading in the original (Ruth 2–4). They marry and begin a family in Bethlehem, and their son, Obed, becomes King David's grandfather and a link to the Messiah Himself.

If, as 1 Corinthians 10:11 tells us, Ruth and Boaz's story is an example for us, written for our instruction, then what should we glean from this story? It's inspiring to see that God included Ruth and several other non-Jews in the lineage of Jesus, which emphasizes that God always had all of us in mind in His plan of salvation. The details of Boaz and Ruth's story also have much to teach us about God's providence in meeting the needs of people who are faithful to Him and the wise choices that invite His provision. Naomi, Ruth, and Boaz all made real choices in this story that affected the outcome.

If we look only for the romantic magic, we miss the underlying wisdom and careful decision-making that invited God's providence. It may seem in retrospect that Jesus' lineage hung in the balance of the spark between a young widow and a possible husband, but the Bible makes it clear that God would have worked His plan through other circumstances if this match had not occurred. As you read the book of Ruth, note each careful, intentional decision that led to the happy outcome. This isn't a story of fate, coincidences, or discovering God's hidden plan; it's the story of faithful people making wise choices, and God pouring His favor on them.

One of the core principles of God's sovereign work in history was articulated by a wise man named Mordecai. In the book of Esther, Mordecai challenged his cousin, Queen Esther, to make a bold decision to defend her people, the Jews: **"For if you keep silent at this time, relief and deliverance will rise for the Jews from another place, but you and your father's house will perish. And who knows whether you have not come to the kingdom for such a time as this?"** (Esther 4:14). God never runs out of options. Just because we can see the awesome sovereignty of God seizing upon our decisions to advance His purposes doesn't mean that God would have somehow been stymied if those choices hadn't been made. Can we foil God's sovereign plan? No! Can we back Him into a corner? Never! God's sovereign will and His Word are not limited at all by the choices that we make.

> God never runs out of options.

Steps for Wise Decision-making

Just because the Bible doesn't clearly spell out some decisions doesn't mean God hasn't given us guidelines for our personal choices. A biblical approach to wise decision-making in matters of personal choice will involve certain steps. Knowing and taking these steps transforms what seems to be a confusing problem into a clear decision. Here in chapter 6, we will outline the steps, and in chapters 7 and 8 we will explore how the steps look in practice, applying the wisdom of Scripture to the reality of personal decision-making.

Step #1: Eliminate unbiblical options.

This may seem like a no-brainer, but I'm amazed by how often Christians trip themselves up in decision-making by including options that directly violate Scripture. Singles who tell me they want to make a godly decision about their marriage partner but date non-Christians endanger their opportunity to make a wise choice. God's Word teaches and illustrates the principle that a shared faith commitment is at the heart of a strong marriage. If the relationship between Christ and His church is the pattern for a marriage (Eph. 5:22–33), then how can the pattern be followed if one of the partners has no relationship with Christ? A Christian who chooses a Christian mate from a field of mixed candidates is showing suspect judgment. The fact that non-believers were under consideration makes the process more reckless than wise.

Wise decision-making begins by being a student of God's Word. Because it is the written expression of God's will, we can confidently rule out choices that would violate its directions. In those instances, we can definitively say, "According to God's Word, this is not God's will for me." In order to make wise decisions, both our heads and our hearts must be in God's

Word. Psalm 119:11 puts it clearly: **"I have stored up your word in my heart, that I might not sin against you."**

This has to be an ongoing process, not a desperate measure we take only when we have to make a decision. The person whose life exemplifies wisdom will also be someone whose **"delight is in the law of the LORD, and on his law he meditates day and night"** (Ps. 1:2). Paul echoes this counsel to Timothy when he writes, **"Do your best to present yourself to God as one approved, a worker who has no need to be ashamed, rightly handling the word of truth"** (2 Tim. 2:15). The way we handle the word of truth, conforming our lives and choices to God's Word, has a direct connection to the way we please God.

Let's consider another big decision: where to go to college. This is a big, haunting choice, so it comes up frequently in discussions of God's will. Does God have a specific college in His will for you to attend? According to our study of biblical decision-making, the answer is no, but He does care very much about the decision you make, and He wants to bless you and give you wisdom in the process.

Following step #1 in biblical decision-making, you identify some criteria that would eliminate a college from consideration in the first place. If a college were likely to cripple you spiritually or put you in a really dark, immoral climate, would that be the best place for you? Does God want you to go to a college where you would be required to live in a coed dorm where roommates pressure you to join in immoral activities? Would enrolling yourself in a setting like that be a healthy decision for a follower of Jesus? Nothing in Scripture suggests such a decision would be wise. Not only would you be placing yourself in a setting of continual temptation, but you would also be inviting abuse and ridicule as you tried to live holy in such an environment. Observation and experience tell me that choosing to put yourself in that position would be foolish. Sadly, some people spend their whole lives recovering from such a foolish decision.

According to 1 Corinthians 6:18, we're supposed to flee temptation, not purposely put ourselves in its pathway! If you have no means to avoid the temptation, look to God for victory, but never make a decision to force the proximity of temptation when it isn't necessary. God wants us to use the wisdom He provides to avoid decisions that require continually asking, "Lord, help me survive in this place." The best option for surviving is choosing not to put yourself there in the first place.

Where the Bible is explicit, the choices are clear, even if they are not easy. Where the Bible gives no specific word, we must use biblical principles. The better we know Scripture, the more clearly we will immediately spot unbiblical options we can eliminate.

When Kathy and I were in seminary, we prayed that God would allow us to serve one church for an entire lifetime, never realizing how difficult that would actually be. At many points along the way, when hardship was high and ministry joy was difficult to find, I looked for an exit ramp that would promise relief from the pain of the moment. However, I was guided and constrained by Psalm 15:4, which was shown to me long ago by a man who had made similar commitments to longevity in a single ministry. God commends the one **"who swears to his own hurt and does not change"** (Ps. 15:4). This is a treasured part of my understanding of God's will. God wants me to keep the promises I've made—even when it's hurtful to do so. As I write this, I'm so glad that portion of God's Word has kept me in God's will.

The pages of our Bibles ought to be dog-eared and filled with notes from the times we have pored over God's Word searching for wisdom.

Step #2: Pray for God's wisdom.

Even after eliminating the unbiblical options, we are often left with a mind-boggling assortment of choices. It's easy to feel overwhelmed. But that can actually be a good response if it drives us to pray for wisdom. I love James's advice: **"If any of you lacks wisdom, let him ask God, who gives generously to all without reproach, and it will be given him"** (James 1:5). What a timely promise!

During my college years, it was hard to pay the bills. I would have loved it if my dad had said, "If you need tuition, just ask." He never said that; he wasn't in a position to make that kind of blanket offer. But God says it, and He can do it. God offers, "If you lack wisdom, just ask!" Faced with bewildering choices, we can pray, "Lord, look at all these choices. I don't have a clue. I need wisdom!" As soon as we realize we need wisdom, we should instantly turn to the One who is all-wise and ask for His help. Not only do we have His permission to ask, but James reassures us how God gives: generously! It's as if our Father says, "You need some wisdom? I'm so glad you asked! Here, have a lot. Take some extra!" God gives wisdom generously and **"without reproach."** The word *reproach* literally means, "He won't sink His teeth into the person who asks." God's gift doesn't come with a bite. When we go to God and ask Him for wisdom, we find Him waiting and willing.

This amazing offer comes in the context of our relationship with God. God's not running a drive-through window, so we can zip by any time for a quick order of understanding with a side of insight. That's not the way God longs to relate to us—only in a crisis. That's not the setting in which we can expect to experience His gift of wisdom.

Parents can immediately relate to God's desire for intimacy. How would parents feel if their child came to them one evening and said, "Mom and Dad, after my siblings go to sleep tonight, I'd like to sit down with you for a few minutes. I have some questions I want to ask you." That would get parents' attention! What if their child continued, "I'm trying to decide about a friend, and I need some wisdom. I mean, you have been living a lot longer than I have, and God's shown you things that I don't know about. Could you just share with me what you've learned about choosing and keeping friends? Could you give me some insight? Could you pray with me about this?" How would parents feel if that happened to them? That's how God feels when we come to Him and ask for wisdom. We know it pleases Him. Might God be thinking, *How amazing! They know they need Me. I have what they want, and they want it too?*

Consider James 3:17: **"But the wisdom from above is first pure, then peaceable, gentle, open to reason, full of mercy and good fruits, impartial and sincere."** Where can you find pure wisdom, nothing else added, no human opinion, no manipulation or hidden agenda? There's only one source that can supply that kind of wisdom. Notice the other qualities of the wisdom God gives:

- It's **"peaceable"**—loves peace. This wisdom rests easily upon you. That's its gentleness.
- God's brand of wisdom is **"open to reason"**—it carefully weighs the truth.
- That openness to reason is balanced by God's wisdom being **"full of mercy and good fruits"**—it's wisdom that accepts people and yields good results. Good things happen in your life when you get and act on God's wisdom.

• Lastly, God's wisdom is **"impartial and sincere."** Which of His children does God prefer? None. He doesn't play favorites, and His gift of wisdom to us is not only impartial but also sincere—without a hidden motive.

Now that's the kind of wisdom we need, and we know where we can get it.

When we ask God for wisdom, we shouldn't merely expect a rush of common sense. Common sense is a good thing; wisdom blows common sense away. Common sense is some human smattering of wisdom that's been picked up through the ages of human observations. God, however, has all the manufacturer's specifications for human happiness, not just a little collection of observations. Earthly common sense has an element of wisdom, but by comparison, God's thoughts about life far exceed common sense (1 Cor. 3:19).

What are some of the areas where we need godly wisdom, not just common sense? Several come to mind immediately.

We should ask God for wisdom to rightly order our priorities. Many worthy voices and needs call for our attention. How do we schedule our activities and efforts without God's truth?

We need wisdom to see the danger beneath the surface of what seems safe. We can pray that for our children, that welling up inside them will be a healthy sense of fear that helps steer them from harm.

We need wisdom to see beyond our experience, wisdom even beyond our years. Again, we can pray this for our children as well as for ourselves. Whenever we face uncharted territory, asking God for wisdom ought to be our first response.

We need wisdom to understand how a decision will affect other areas of life. Sometimes we compartmentalize our choices, thinking we can get away with a choice in one area without effects in the other areas. But God can help us realize a choice's far-reaching effects on our life goals and loved ones.

We need wisdom to see how things are connected. A quality that marks a wise person is the ability to make unexpected connections and see patterns of truth that others can't recognize on their own.

We need wisdom to keep away from things that might enslave or destroy us.

When do we ever *not* need wisdom? Asking God for wisdom should be one of our prayer habits, as well as a request in specific situations when we have a heightened awareness of our need.

Step #3: Yield to the Holy Spirit's leading.

Jesus didn't leave us as orphans. He gave us a Helper to be with us forever, to lead us through life on this earth (John 14:16–18). Is God's Spirit trying to keep us on a tightly monitored sequence of choices that we are supposed to follow perfectly? No, the Holy Spirit does not lead us according to a detailed plan; He does lead us away from foolishness and toward wisdom. Because God loves us and wants to protect us from true harm, He promises wisdom and also provides leading. Again, God has no divine need to guide every choice we make; rather, in a healthy relationship with Him, we maintain a continual desire to yield to the Holy Spirit's leading whenever there's a choice God signals is best for us.

Jesus said, **"Behold, I have set before you an open door, which no one is able to shut"** (Rev. 3:8). Sometimes God opens the way before us as we seek His wisdom. According to Romans 8:14, **"For all who are led by the Spirit of God are sons of God."** How many people are led by the Spirit of God? Every one of His children. Every single one is being led, directed, and guided by the Spirit of God into making wise choices.

How does the leading of the Holy Spirit and the yielding by us happen? I have observed that we sometimes misunderstand the Holy Spirit's leading and make it very subjective. We cease to practice what the Bible describes as God's leading when we turn His Spirit into a puppet-master and ourselves into mindless puppets. John 16:13 tells us, **"When the Spirit of truth comes, he will guide you into all the truth, for he will not speak on his own authority, but whatever he hears he will speak, and he will declare to you the things that are to come."** Where does the Holy Spirit guide us? Into the truth! Would you have ever realized you needed a Savior if the Holy

Spirit hadn't guided you into that truth? We can count on the Holy Spirit's guidance, even if that truth is, in some cases, a God-approved choice between two equally good options. Jesus added, **"He will glorify me, for he will take what is mine and declare it to you"** (John 16:14). The ministry of the Spirit is to remind us of the Word of God and to guide us into a wise application of what God's Word actually says.

The Spirit reminds us of the truth. **"But the Helper, the Holy Spirit, whom the Father will send in my name, he will teach you all things and bring to your remembrance all that I have said to you"** (John 14:26). Countless times in my life, a verse that I had memorized or studied in depth has come back to my mind at a critical moment—if not word-perfect then at least the sense of it. I have remembered enough to dig through the Scriptures, find the passage, and get wisdom for the decision at hand.

This doctrine is the illuminating ministry of the Holy Spirit. That ministry of the Holy Spirit involves opening our eyes, lighting our paths, and guiding our way. The Spirit of God draws our attention to the Word of God. Anyone who wants to live wisely must yield to the Holy Spirit's ministry of illuminating the words of Scripture.

> The Spirit of God draws our attention to the Word of God.

When Kathy and I first moved to the Chicago area, nearly thirty years ago, we came to start seminary and had just enough money to cover one semester's expenses. Pulling up stakes from our home in Canada was a huge decision. But we checked with several trusted advisors, especially the pastor of the church where we were serving, and they encouraged us to move forward and trust that God would provide. We were discovering that walking in wisdom doesn't necessarily eliminate the feeling of risk!

We sold our house, but the exchange rate coming south made our small profit much smaller. When we got to Chicago, we watched our bank account rapidly dwindle as I started school. As Canadians, Kathy and I had student visas but not work visas, so we technically couldn't even get jobs here. But while we were packing the truck to move, a church in the Chicago suburbs called us and asked me to interview for their singles' pastor position that they had been trying to fill for a whole year. We feared they would never want to go through the hassle of getting our visas updated, but the Lord laid it on their hearts to hire us, and God met all of our financial needs.

I firmly believe God led in all that. Do I believe that's the only place we could have gone? No. Do I believe if we had gone somewhere else that God wouldn't have provided for us, and our whole lives would have been a travesty? No. But we tried to make wise decisions, to trust God, and to follow His leading. We must never forget that while we're making decisions and taking actions, so is God! The step of learning to yield to the Holy Spirit's guidance will faithfully deliver good results.

Step #4: Weigh heavily the consensus of godly counsel.

Want some wisdom about wisdom? **"Plans are established by counsel"** (Prov. 20:18). If you want to make a good decision, then eliminate the unbiblical options, pray for wisdom, yield to the Holy Spirit, and solicit good counsel. Go to some people you respect, who are known for wisdom, and ask their advice. "I'm thinking about situation or opportunity X. I've been preparing to make a wise decision than honors God. Here's what I have considered. Have I overlooked anything? How do you believe God might be guiding me in this decision? What would please Him? What would be wise?" These are important questions to ask. Give those advisors enough background to see the whole picture.

> We must never forget that while we're making decisions and taking actions, so is God!

When it comes to soliciting godly counsel, here are some wrong approaches:

Going to only one person. Don't get counsel from one person; get counsel from several people. Often, you will discover that what at first looks like a decision between two good choices is more accurately a decision between a good choice and a better choice.

Going to people until you get the answer you want. This is a particularly dangerous strategy if the first person you go to agrees with your tentative decision. It isn't bad to keep asking until you find at least one person who sees the situation very differently. Ultimately you may not follow that advice, but you will know you've received a balanced perspective and looked at the decision from multiple angles. As you go through life, identify a circle of trusted counselors. These are people who offer proven, wise counsel and do not hesitate to question your thinking or motives.

Going to people who are not known for wisdom. If their lives are a train wreck, you probably don't want to check in with them on your decisions. This would be like asking for financial advice from a person in bankruptcy or marital advice from a person with a string of broken marriages. Instead, seek out people who are known for wisdom, such as elders and church leaders who have offered to be available to you. They are often perceived as spiritual mentors available only to comfort and pray with you, but they are also valuable resources for decision-making. Ask them, "Does anything come to mind from God's Word regarding my decision about X? Do you have any wisdom to share about this choice? I want to be wise and please God with my choice."

Step #5: Trust God's sovereignty to use all wise decisions for your good.

None of us makes decisions perfectly. And a good decision should never be measured solely by its short-term results. Sometimes the wise, good, and right decision leads to a very difficult time, but God is at work. **"For it is God who works in you, both to will and to work for his good pleasure"** (Phil. 2:13). In other words, the very desire rising within you to make choices that would please God is being stirred by Him. This will flow as you lay your decisions open before Him and pray, "God, I want my life to please You. I want to make a wise choice in this matter. I will not pursue my own agenda or my own needs. I want what You would want and what would honor You."

Sometimes, what would please God is what would please you. Those are easy decisions! God is ready to give us the go-ahead with our choices. But sometimes a choice that pleases God doesn't particularly please us. Or we can't see that it will please us because we have a limited perspective. Wisdom doesn't necessarily feel good. But wisdom is not a dot to stand on or a straight line to meticulously follow. It's not the right choice vs. the wrong choice. God's way of living involves the wise choice that will please the Lord. Live in the lush green pastures within the fences of God's Word. Make wise choices that please God, and trust that He is at work in you **"to will and to work for his good pleasure"** (Phil. 2:13).

Sometimes God allows us to make choices that on a human level don't seem to have been the best. He might allow us to buy a home with hidden problems or a car that breaks down. Sometimes we pray for wisdom and make a decision that seems right but doesn't pan out. The situation may be hard, yet God's sovereignty extends even to those areas, provided that we've sought to make a wise choice that would please Him.

If we don't care what God says and make haphazard choices on a whim, then God's Word has some faithful reminders for us. If we sow the wind, we will reap the whirlwind (Hosea 8:7). But if we tried to make a wise decision, if we sought to please the Lord, God's Word tells us that even those things that don't work out will eventually work out. **"And we know that for those who love God all things work together for good, for those who are called according to his purpose"** (Rom. 8:28). If your motivation was to honor God and you sought to make the wisest choice possible, then God's sovereignty extends to all things and makes them work together for your good.

Would you rather live a life in which you second-guess every decision you made, in which you have to perfectly make every decision in a razor's edge sequence of decisions God plotted out for you?

Or would you prefer to live the kind of abundant life that Jesus lived and promised, where choices are real, and

God doesn't control every decision you make? God promises wisdom for decision-making—and God always keeps His promises.

Sovereign God,

 You are in control, and You are good, so I can trust You. Always. All true wisdom flows from You (Prov. 9:10). Father, I love You, and I want to please You, and I know that desire in and of itself is pleasing to You. I know that my vision is limited, and I need Your wisdom to see and choose what's best. Please lead me to others who will speak wisdom into my life too. Thank You that You promise to give me wisdom generously, and You always keep Your promises. In Jesus' name I pray. Amen.

CHAPTER 7

Decision Time—Part One

EVERY WEEK, I stare into the eyes of people who live with regrets. Most Sundays, if I ask the question, "How many people here realize they have made some really garbage decisions in their lives?" I hear instant laughter of agreement. The question levels people. The details vary, but we all have some version of the same past. Bad decisions in our wake remind us we're all in the same boat. Maybe that realization is the beginning of true community.

People who live with the traditional view of God's will have to endure the crushing weight of regrets. Not only do they realize they have made mistakes and bad decisions, but they also have to cope with the idea that they have fallen out of God's perfect will, meaning that the best they can hope for is a poor alternate plan. These haunted people can hardly imagine God looking at them with compassion. Instead, their minds are filled with worrisome thoughts: *Is God furrowing His brow at me again? Has God turned His face away from me yet? My life can never be what it would/could/should have been, if only I had been able to figure out and stick to His perfect will.* No wonder the church is filled with so many unhappy Christians!

But if we are willing to make the shift from the traditional view of God's will to what He has revealed in His Word, then every day can be a fresh challenge to apply God's principles to make wise decisions. Instead of seeing regrets as evidence of irreversible damage in the past, we can simply see them as reminders to do better today and tomorrow. We can leave the past in God's hands and focus on today's decisions. We can resolve, "I may have made some wrong choices and committed some grievous sins in my yesterdays, but today I choose to draw close to Him and to look to my future. I choose to believe I can experience God's best in my life for the rest of my days, if I'll live in submission to Him, regardless of what lies behind me."

Does this describe you yet? Do you share these convictions?

- God's will is not a narrow sequence of choices.
- God's will is a lush, green pasture within the fences of His Word.
- God isn't limited by your choices.
- God actually gives you a great deal of freedom to roam and graze all over the pasture.

Instead of taking on the impossibility of being responsible for the maintenance of God's perfect will, you can begin to relax into the more reasonable idea of being responsible for your own life before God.

If that describes your thinking, then the rest of the book will make sense in the context of this new framework, and we can begin looking at practical applications: how this looks in real life. If you're still struggling to shake the traditional view of God's will, then you may want to reread some earlier portions of the book before you move to the next phase.

If, as our framework suggests, there are good choices, not just one choice, the point of tension shifts a little. Here's a typical response:

"This new level of personal freedom and responsibility makes me nervous. Even though I've tried to read the Bible faithfully, it's a big book, and there's a lot of stuff in there. What if there's some obscure passage in Ezekiel with the key insight I needed—and I missed it? I thought I was inside those parameters of God's will, but I didn't know the whole book. Aren't there some overriding principles I can go by to make wise decisions? Aren't there some basic biblical principles that lead to wise choices, rules of thumb I can use that will increase the likelihood that my decisions please God?"

Yes, there are! In fact, let's consider together nine decision-making principles that create a great framework for making wise choices. These can be arranged into three sets of three, making them easier to remember.

Spiritual considerations—the God check

Relational considerations—the boat check

Internal considerations—the gut check

These principles will help you evaluate your decisions in the light of your relationship with God, your relationships with others ("How will this choice affect my relationships with other believers?"), and your personal integrity ("How will this choice affect me as a person, who I am and what I'm becoming?").

> These nine questions distill the vast wisdom of the Bible into some specific, point-of-action checks.

These nine questions distill the vast wisdom of the Bible into some specific, point-of-action checks. We will spend the bulk of chapter 7 on the first category, spiritual considerations, and explore relational considerations and internal considerations in chapter 8.

Spiritual Considerations (The God Check)

This is the perfect place to begin: the God check.

There are three questions I have found crucial in checking my relationship with God before I make decisions. Even if I'm in a tight spot and have a pressing choice to make, I still want to take enough time to make a wise decision that will please my heavenly Father. So I've learned to use these three considerations, which act like a spiritual grid for my choices.

The first "God check" question is this: ***Will this choice bring glory to God?***

Let's look at an example of this question in context. Welcome to the church in Corinth, recipient of two of Paul's New Testament letters. This church was a quagmire of bad decisions. They peppered Paul with questions and made horrendous decisions that he had to confront. As a church, they denied the blatant sins of some of their members, and they developed sinful behaviors that extended even to their corporate worship and the way they approached the Lord's Supper. But their raging problem related to meat offered to idols.

Corinth was one of the most pluralistically pagan cities in the ancient world. Religion was big business. Non-Christians would arrange for animal sacrifices at the temple to atone for certain sins or to gain favor with the gods. Religion was even part of doing business. Sacrifices were sometimes included in business deals.

The sacrificial system had two parts: the killing of the animal and the offering of the edible by-products. Choice cuts of meat were laid out before the gods. The pagan priests developed a thriving side business in the meat market. After the penitents left, the priests would sell the meat out the back door of the temple to enterprising merchants, who then sold the meat to the public.

Everyone knew these chops and steaks were recycled sacrifices. This created a dilemma for Christians, who wanted no part of the pagan sacrifices yet knew those sacrifices to lifeless idols were meaningless. The Christians were buzzing about this issue. It was just the kind of topic people could really sink their teeth into!

Some reasoned, "We should never eat meat that was offered to idols. It has been spiritually tainted. This meat is horrible!"

Others argued, "There's only one, true God, who sacrificed His Son once and for all. These idols are just fancy pieces of metal, stone, and wood, so the meat is just meat. Let's eat." The apostle Paul took this position, but his teaching did not prevent an uproar in the church. This set the stage for Paul to teach a deeper principle about settling disputes over choices. To the Corinthian Christians (and to us), Paul wrote, **"'All things are lawful,' but not all things are helpful. 'All things are lawful,' but not all things build up. Let no one seek his own good, but the good of his neighbor"** (1 Cor. 10:23–24).

In other words, it's not always right to do what is within your right to do. Others are involved. It doesn't necessarily help others if you're only interested in helping yourself. Paul explained his teaching in the context of meat, and then he gave this powerful summary statement: **"So, whether you eat or drink, or whatever you do, do all to the glory of God"** (1 Cor. 10:31).

This is the first principle in wise decision-making. Our decisions don't boil down to meaningless preferences about food, drink, and other minutiae; they boil down to giving glory to God.

Today, Christians might not be bent out of shape about meat offered to idols. At least, I've never heard that discussed in the lobby of our church. But just like the church in Corinth, every church has issues. Put more than a handful of Christians in the same place, and some big and little issues will certainly emerge. Christians wonder, "What's the right way? What's a good decision? On which topics do Christians have to be in complete agreement?" The guiding principle is still the same today, even though the issues are different. And it begins with this standard: **"So, whether you eat or drink, or whatever you do, do all to the glory of God"** (1 Cor. 10:31).

This idea of doing all to the glory of God should be the consuming passion of people who claim to follow Jesus Christ. Everything He did was for the glory of God, so we dare not set our sights on some lesser target.

What is His glory? Glory is to God as wet is to water, as heat is to fire, as light is to bulb. Glory is what emanates from God. Glory is the weight of God's presence. So if God were here and we recognized His presence, it would not be because any of us can see God (John 1:18). What we see is God's glory, the evidence that He is here. All creation shouts His glory: **"The heavens declare the glory of God, and the sky above proclaims his handiwork"** (Ps. 19:1).

Some moments in life, God's glory is so obvious to us. Have you ever had this experience? Standing on a seashore at night, glimpsing infinity in the waves. Staring into the starry sky. Witnessing the birth of a child. Experiencing the size of the Grand Canyon, the power of Niagara Falls, the beauty of a sunset. In those moments, we're struck with the realization, *Wow, there must be a God.* Filled with awe, we would never conclude that all of this came about by accident. The wonder of it all tells us there is a God. That's when we feel Psalm 19:1.

> Glory is to God as wet is to water, as heat is to fire, as light is to bulb. Glory is what emanates from God.

Those who suppress that recognition of God's glory, who claim that all of this is meaningless coincidence, have a deliberate agenda. They violate their own better judgment. Sooner or later, everyone will be forced to acknowledge the truth. All of creation will echo the shout of God's glory. **"Therefore God has highly exalted him and bestowed on him the name that is above every name, so that at the name of Jesus every knee should bow, in heaven and on earth and under the earth, and every tongue confess that Jesus Christ is Lord, to the glory of God the Father"** (Phil. 2:9–11). One way or another, everyone will give glory to God. We might as well keep practicing here and now!

And at the top of God's list entitled "Stuff That Brings Me Glory" is "My children." Just as creation shouts God's glory, so should our lives. **"Or do you not know that your body is a temple of the Holy Spirit within you, whom you have from God? You are not your own, for you were bought with a price. So glorify God in your body"** (1 Cor. 6:19–20). God wants His children to manifest His presence, to bring glory to Him, to show that He is real. If you're His child, the reason God gives you another breath is so that as you move through life, you can make choices that show He is real and alive and that bring glory to Him.

It's worth noting that this doesn't suggest God has an unhealthy desire for attention. It's all about what we were designed to do—to bring glory to God. Our central purpose in life, our number one reason for existing, is to bring glory to God. It's not something God needs; it's something *we* need to do in order to fulfill our ultimate purpose.

Our decisions show the reality of God in our lives. Let's say you face a choice between Option A and Option B. Option A falls squarely within the guidelines of God's Word, the choice that someone who cares deeply about what God thinks would make. Option B is a selfish, "I'm-going-to-do-what-I-want-to-do" choice with instant, short-term gratification. When you make the difficult choice, others see that decision and ask, "Why would you possibly choose Option A?" The answer is, of course, "Because I want to please God." Those decisions show how much weight God has with us, and our choices reflect His glory.

So when I want to make a wise choice, at the top of my list is this question: Will my particular choice bring glory to God? Will it show that God holds the place of top priority in my life?

The second "God check" question is this: *Is this a decision Jesus would make?*

Every day of His packed, three-year public ministry, Jesus made choices. The Gospels clearly depict how decisive Jesus was. He didn't hesitate, second-guess, or spend time regretting decisions He had made. One of the primary motivations for becoming intimately acquainted with Jesus' life is so that we can check our decisions against His pattern. **"For to this you have been called, because Christ also suffered for you, leaving you an example, so that you might follow in his steps"** (1 Pet. 2:21).

What would it look like to truly **"follow in his steps"**? If we really are followers of the Lord Jesus, our lives ought to look like His. How can we show the world that we are simply, plainly, and persistently followers of the Lord Jesus Christ? The very name we bear, *Christians*, means "little Christs" and was used to mock the early disciples' desire to be living copies of the original (Acts 11:26). The insult stuck and became a fitting description of those who take following Jesus seriously. They imitate Christ.

This is the constant challenge for Christians. Where would Jesus walk? If He would step over there, then we will step over there. If He would make this choice, then we will make this choice. Simple to explain, difficult to execute.

More than a century ago, Charles Sheldon wrote a novel called *In His Steps*, which became one of the best-selling books of all time. The story centers on a pastor, Henry Maxwell, who stumbles over the seriousness of the idea of imitating Christ in everyday life. Maxwell got fired up about following in Jesus' steps, and He challenged others to ask the question, "What would Jesus do?" The vision spread like wildfire, in the lives of individuals, through the church, spilling over into the whole city.

What if it weren't fiction? What if Christ-representatives actually lived like the Christ?

> What if Christ-representatives actually lived like the Christ?

When people get serious about following Jesus, they always draw others into their wake.

Our inner cynics remind us that Jesus lived two thousand years ago—how are we supposed to know what He would do in any given situation? As 1 Peter 2:21 told us, He left us a pattern, not a verbatim script. Jesus faced situations like the situations we face and responded to them in ways that give us clues for our own responses. The four Gospels are filled with stories of Jesus, and Acts describes the first efforts to walk in His steps. As we read the stories, we have to look for clues.

- What did Jesus do when He felt disappointed with people?
- What did Jesus do when He had to trust God?
- How did He handle criticism?
- How did Jesus handle the betrayal of a close friend?
- What did He do when He saw wrongs being committed?

Study the Gospels for Jesus' practical response patterns. If we are serious about being His followers, we can immerse ourselves in His stories and imitate His responses. We have a lot to learn, but the guidance we need is right there in God's Word.

When Jesus was criticized, He answered directly, simply, without offense, and generally only once (see Matt. 27:11–14).

When Jesus felt exhausted and weighed down with the pressures of people and circumstances, He got away and got alone and sought the refreshment of His fellowship with God the Father. **"But he would withdraw to desolate places and pray"** (Luke 5:16).

When Jesus was betrayed by a close friend, He didn't react out of hurt. He didn't fly off the handle or justify hurtful words and actions because He was hearing and experiencing them. He accepted the pain with resignation and trusted in His ultimate vindication (see John 13:21–30).

While Jesus certainly turned the other cheek to those who maligned Him, when He saw others mistreated, He spoke up. He handled injustice toward others aggressively. (See Christ's bold reaction to how the religious leaders were abusing the people in the temple in Mark 11:15–18.)

When we try to imitate Christ, it isn't a one-size-fits-all answer for every situation. Sometimes Jesus had all the time in the world for people, but when in His humanity His personal resources were depleted, He didn't hesitate to raise a boundary and pull away until He was replenished. He didn't use the inexhaustible resources of His deity to cover the limits of His humanity.

Might we choose to **"follow in his steps"**?

If we want to make wise choices, we start by asking ourselves the questions, "Will this choice bring glory to God?" and "Is this a decision Jesus would make?" The third "God check" question is this: *Will I be proud of this decision at the judgment seat of Christ?*

This question brings the view from heaven into our daily lives. It's tempting to make decisions based solely on immediate circumstances rather than stepping back and seeing our choices in the light of eternity. How willing are we to view replays of our decisions while standing next to Jesus Christ in heaven? **"Why do you pass judgment on your brother? Or you, why do you despise your brother? For we will all stand before the judgment seat of God; for it is written, 'As I live, says the Lord, every knee shall bow to me, and every tongue shall confess to God.' So then each of us will give an account of himself to God"** (Rom. 14:10–12).

When it comes to caution in decision-making, the key phrase in this passage is this: **"For we will all stand before the judgment seat of God"** (14:10). We will all stand with Christ for an instant replay of history. You'll be there. People who have wronged you will be there. People you have wronged will be there. I'll be there. It will not be a flippant moment. It will be serious, up close, and personal. Can you imagine standing before the Lord God Almighty, and as those scenes from your life are replayed, looking into the eyes of the Lord Jesus and accounting for each choice, for every idle word? We have to live with a sense of the weight of that moment.

That future, unavoidable life screening doesn't have to be some horrible, tragic thing. We have the opportunity to make choices now. We can ask the "God check" questions now, before it's too late. Imagine how differently those moments will feel if the Lord asks, "Why did you choose that?" with a smile on His face, and you can answer, "Because I wanted to please You, Lord. I didn't feel like making that choice at the time, but I knew it was the right choice. It was terribly difficult, but You gave me the strength, and afterward, I saw the blessing that came from it." Even though we won't be proud of everything we've done, that accounting before the Lord can be a wonderful thing!

As we make choices in life, we can persistently ask, "Will this bring glory to God?" If I have settled the issue that life is not ultimately about me but about Him, then I can address that question sincerely.

And if I've settled the fact that doing things Jesus' way is the best way, then I can ask, "Is this a decision Jesus would make?"

And I can ask, "Will I be proud of this decision at the judgment seat of Christ?" I don't want to be ashamed of how I've used all the privileges God entrusted to me.

Perhaps this is why Paul could write such glowing words to Timothy as he saw his own time on earth coming to a close: **"For I am already being poured out as a drink offering, and the time of my departure has come. I have fought the good fight, I have finished the race, I have kept the faith. Henceforth there is laid up for me the crown of**

**righteousness, which the Lord, the righteous judge, will
award to me on that Day, and not only to me but also to all
who have loved his appearing"** (2 Tim. 4:6–8). These are the
words of a person who has chosen wisely and is eager to see
Christ, not someone who is dreading accountability.

If we run our decisions first through the spiritual grid (the
God check), then we will eliminate a lot of wrong or weak
options from the start. Even between several perfectly acceptable options, the God check questions will often clarify which
of the choices has the best chance of pleasing God (and us)
when we review the reels of our lives.

In chapter 8, we will explore the relational considerations
(the boat check) and personal considerations (the gut check)
of decision-making. Even after clarifying God's perspective
on your choices, you need to consider how your choices affect
other people. You're not an island. You don't live in a vacuum,
and God cares about the decisions you make and how they
affect others. Once you have checked your choices in the light
of God's priorities and the needs of other people in your life,
then you can consider your personal feelings.

Remember, this pattern of checks is counterintuitive to
the world. Many people consult their own feelings and desires
before they consider what God thinks or how their choices
will affect others. (You may recognize that habit in yourself.)
"Follow your heart," "do what feels right," and "live in the

moment" all sound appealing at first, but our hearts are rotten leaders.

The most glaring reason why many Christians make such poor decisions is because they check with God as an afterthought. The One who knows best is treated as a last resort. In fact, sometimes we don't do a God check of our decisions until after we've made them and things have gone terribly awry. If we want to live wisely, we will first seek to find Christ's footsteps in a similar situation and then try to place our feet in the very same spots.

My Father,

Thank You not only for revealing wisdom in Your Word but also for Your Son's "footprints" in the Gospels. I want to walk as Jesus walked. When I feel burdened by life's choices, I want to come to You and find rest for my soul. Teach me to live in that intimate relationship with You. Thank You for always walking ahead of me, beside me, and behind me every step of the way (Ps. 139:5). In the name of the Lord Jesus and for Your glory alone. Amen.

CHAPTER 8

Decision Time—Part Two

HOW DO WE ensure we're making wise decisions? By asking ourselves a series of questions that embody biblical wisdom. In chapter 7, we introduced the three God check questions:

1. *Will this choice bring glory to God?*
2. *Is this a decision Jesus would make?*
3. *Will I be proud of this decision at the judgment seat of Christ?*

After we have given God an opportunity to overrule and direct our decisions, we still have two more areas of concern we need to consider as we make choices: the boat check (relational considerations) and the gut check (personal considerations). Even the sequence of these questions is significant. God first! Then others. Lastly me. Our culture encourages us to reverse that order and make decisions solely on personal gut feelings. That approach, when followed consistently, leads to consistently bad choices. When it's decision time, we want to run things by God first before we test them by the next two checks.

The Boat Check

You are not an island. In fact, your choices ripple out and affect those in proximity to you. If you want to make wise decisions, you have to consider the relational angle.

Paul reminds us, **"'All things are lawful,' but not all things are helpful. 'All things are lawful,' but not all things build up. Let no one seek his own good, but the good of his neighbor"** (1 Cor. 10:23–24). In other words, don't just consider how this choice affects you; how does it affect those around you?

As humans, we're in a common boat. And as Christians, we form a unique fellowship (pun intended) that we can preserve or damage by the choices we make.

Many people embrace the Golden Rule (though many don't realize who articulated that very rule: Jesus Christ). **"So whatever you wish that others would do to you, do also to them, for this is the Law and the Prophets"** (Matt. 7:12). How do you want others to treat you? That's how you should treat others. Let's apply that to decision-making. Do you want others to consider how their choices will affect you? Of course! Then you should consider others as you make choices. That seems fair. Before making a decision, you should ask yourself,

"If I make this choice, will someone get tossed overboard? Will this cause a leak in the ship? Will it cause the boat to run aground or to crash into rocks?"

As we examine how our choices will affect others, we can distill biblical teaching into three good relational questions. The first boat check question is this: *Would I want this done to me?*

Paul's teaching clearly supports the idea of the Golden Rule. **"Owe no one anything, except to love each other, for the one who loves another has fulfilled the law. For the commandments, 'You shall not commit adultery, You shall not murder, You shall not steal, You shall not covet,' and any other commandment, are summed up in this word: 'You shall love your neighbor as yourself.' Love does no wrong to a neighbor; therefore love is the fulfilling of the law"** (Rom. 13:8–10). Paul tells us to avoid all forms of debt except one—to owe other people love.

None of us loves from scratch. We love because we've been loved. Long before we grasp what it means to love or how to love someone back, we were both divinely and humanly loved. When we love others, it may feel like we're initiating something, but the fact is that love is always a response, direct or indirect. We may not be responding directly to the person we are loving, but the love we are expressing is a reflection of the love we have received. **"We love because he first loved us"** (1 John 4:19). Because love is always a game of catch-up, we should consider ourselves in love-debt to God and to our neighbor.

Love encompasses all the relational commandments. Paul ticks off commandments 7, 6, 8, and 10 from God's Top Ten list, and then reminds us that all of those specific commands are **"summed up in this word: 'You shall love your neighbor as yourself'"** (Rom. 13:9).

There's a lot of warped teaching in the church today about the importance of loving yourself. That's not taught in the Bible; it's assumed in the Bible. You already love yourself. Every day when you wake up, your given priority is how to take care of yourself, meet your own needs, pursue your own agenda—that's your intrinsic sin nature. You don't need someone to teach you how to love yourself.

> Because love is always a game of catch-up, we should consider ourselves in love-debt to God and to our neighbor.

People infected with the popular view might argue, "I'm actually really down on myself. I hate myself. Loving myself doesn't come naturally to me." Yet this is just a perverse form of self-love. It's an obsessive focus on self. If you didn't naturally love yourself, then you wouldn't feel badly about how you look or about your achievements.

We need to be set free from that self-centeredness, but the path to freedom from negative self-centeredness is not to focus harder on loving yourself. The way to get free is to love God and to love others. That kind of love is intentional and active. It's not about feelings; it's about actions, specific acts of love toward others.

In a nutshell, love means "you before me." In the realm of decision-making, if I'm going to make wise choices, I must make a point to ask myself, "Would I want this done to me?" Before making a choice, the wise person pauses and meditates, "If I were on the receiving end of this decision, would I want this done to me?"

Sometimes the boat check will cause you to do hard things. To make a selfless choice that's for the ultimate good of another. To move aggressively toward a brother or sister who has fallen spiritually. In the moment, that person might not welcome you or might perceive you as meddlesome, but your intervention might be the ultimate act of love. "If I ever got to that bad place," the loving person reasons, "I would want someone to come after me."

Genuine love rarely requires us to do the gushy, sentimental thing. Love isn't a Hallmark-card thing; it's a take-up-your-cross-and-follow-Me thing (Luke 9:23). Love isn't soft and passive; it's strong and active. If we understand the nature of biblical love, we will treat others as we honestly desire to be treated.

The second boat check question is this: ***Will this decision appear wrong to someone, even though it's right?*** Now this, my friends, really requires us to set aside our own desires.

According to 1 Thessalonians 5:22, we should **"Abstain from every form of evil,"** or in slightly different wording, **"Abstain from all appearance of evil"** (KJV). Not only are we to avoid things that are wrong, but we're also to avoid doing things that might *look* wrong.

This has direction applications to how we love other people. We want to avoid choices that might look wrong to them. This is a hard truth to practice, but if we really want to make decisions that please the Lord, we will factor appearances into our decisions.

Let me share an embarrassing illustration of how challenging this can be, and you can see how I'm trying to live these truths out too.

A few years ago, I had this really cool idea to build a flower box in my backyard. Let me hasten to add that I won't be asked to host an HGTV home improvement show anytime soon. But I had a vision for this flower box, and I knew the perfect spot for it: right behind my neighbor's garage. It was big enough to partly hide my neighbor's old, red brick shed. I thought the ancient masonry would make a great backdrop for the flowers I planned to plant, but I would need to place it very close to his garage. I knew I needed to discuss this with my neighbor so he would have fair warning about my plans.

So I went and talked to him about my grand vision. "Hey, neighbor, I want to run some ideas by you." We have a good relationship, and he was great about the whole thing. Check.

I built this monster flower box, eighteen feet long and almost waist high. I hauled in countless wheelbarrows of dirt until it was filled. When I put the finishing touches on it, I realized with satisfaction that I had created a major flower resting place. Perfect.

Or so I thought. A year passed, and I encountered another man from my neighborhood, who happens to be the brother-in-law of my flower box neighbor. He surprised me with his strong reaction to my masterpiece project. "How could you build that there? Don't you realize it's going to eventually wreck his garage? Moisture is going to seep into the brick, destroy the tuck-pointing, and create a mess." He was all over me about it.

I reviewed the steps I had taken in the project. I had my neighbor's open permission, so I was sure I hadn't done anything wrong. I was tempted to brush the criticism aside, but as the days went by, I kept thinking about the situation. The next time I saw the brother-in-law, he was still really worked up about the flower box. I knew that if I tried to respond to him, I might be tempted to say something defensive, so I just listened carefully. Then I went home and talked to my wife about it. She agreed that I hadn't done anything wrong, and then she smiled and lovingly said, "I know you'll make the wise decision, James."

Who knew I would have to pray about a flower box! Now one natural reaction might be to say, "This is none of your business! My neighbor doesn't have a problem with the flower box. You take care of your property, and I'll take care of mine." But some of these biblical decision-making principles were running through my mind, and I saw that even if I was technically in the clear, if my choice caused someone else to get bent, then it wasn't the right choice.

Without love, we can't even consider that kind of perspective. If we care first and foremost about ourselves, then we will do only what pleases us. But if we want to please God, then we are going to have to get serious about loving others. We may even have to do things that are a major inconvenience.

I ripped out the flower box. It cost me as much money to get it out as it cost me to put it in. But every time I look at the empty space where that flower box used to be, I feel really good about it. Even though I haven't always done this well, this time I knew I had pleased the Lord. I realized that what was important to me (the flower box) was not the most important thing (loving my neighbor). What a prime opportunity to practice what I preach.

If you want to make wise decisions and please the Lord, then you're going to have to consider the relational implications of your choices. That begins by asking yourself, "How will this decision affect other people? Would I want this done to me? Could this appear to be wrong, even if it's right?" Those challenges will always reveal whether or not we have learned to consider others before ourselves.

The third boat check question is this: ***Will this choice cause a brother or sister in Christ to struggle spiritually?***

We live with blinders on. Often we do things and handle ourselves in certain ways and don't realize how we're affecting other people. Most of us can't see ourselves as others see us. I've discovered this repeatedly in my life. I'm sure you have too. You're just going along, doing what you do, and all of a sudden, you become aware that something you did or said hurt someone else spiritually. The clue is often a sudden change in the temperature of the room. You may not know what you said that caused it, but you know that an offense has been committed, and that you are the likely suspect.

Now what? If you really want to make choices that please God, you're going to stop doing what causes others to stumble. You may even have to humbly ask where you went wrong. From God's perspective, the way we affect others is more important than our exercise of personal freedom. Now before we get all offended that God expects so much from us, let's remember that He follows the same standard. Read this description of Jesus: **"Do nothing from selfish ambition or conceit, but in humility count others more significant than yourselves. Let each of you look not only to his own interests, but also to the interests of others. Have this mind among yourselves, which is yours in Christ Jesus, who, though he was in the form of**

God, *did not count equality with God a thing to be grasped*, but emptied himself, by taking the form of a servant, being born in the likeness of men. And being found in human form, he humbled himself by becoming obedient to the point of death, even death on a cross" (Phil. 2:3–8, emphasis mine).

Jesus doesn't ask us to do something He hasn't already done. He is the supreme example of putting others first. Jesus willingly became one of us in order to reach us. He gave up what was rightfully His for our good.

The first two boat check questions—*Would I want this done to me? Will this decision appear wrong to someone, even though it's right?*—have universal application. These relate to how we get along with people in general. Our standard for treating everyone boils down to recognizing how we want to be treated and learning when others might be offended by our choices.

But the third boat check question has to do with avoiding leaks in the fellowship, taking care that we don't thoughtlessly create problems for our fellow travelers on board the ship of faith in Christ.

A whole chunk of Romans 14 spells this out. Paul makes the initial point in verse 13, and the rest of the passage provides illustrations and applications. **"Therefore let us not pass judgment on one another any longer, but rather decide never to put a stumbling block or hindrance in the way of a brother"** (Rom. 14:13). If we've decided never to put a stumbling block in someone's way, then if we discover we unintentionally did, we'll want to remove it quickly.

If Jesus loves these people enough to die for them, then what are we willing to do to express that kind of love for them? Is anything worth causing our spiritual siblings to stumble? Paul challenges us, **"Do not, for the sake of food, destroy the work of God. Everything is indeed clean, but it is wrong for anyone to make another stumble by what he eats. It is good not to eat meat or drink wine or do anything that causes your brother to stumble"** (Rom. 14:20–21). Even if something is good, if it causes someone to stumble, just stop doing it! It's not that important.

We are a selfish bunch of people, and we live in a selfish generation. We are all about our so-called rights! But the concept of making decisions that please God flies right in the face of the

> Is anything worth causing our spiritual siblings to stumble?

spirit of our culture. Making decisions that won't cause other people to struggle spiritually is a standard we resist because we want to do what we want to do! We might be tempted to grumble, "If we have to take God into consideration when we make choices, fine. But if we also have to think about all these weak Christians around us and how our perfectly reasonable choices will affect them, that is going to get really tiring and irritating after a while."

Can you imagine God's reaction to our petty fights? If you're a parent, you have likely watched your children bickering and sighed, "I wish they'd just get along!" I hear parents talk about this all the time. They ask, "How can we get our kids to get along better?" Believe me, I know the feeling. When my wife and I see our kids at odds with each other, it makes us feel lousy. Some of the things kids bicker over are ridiculous! They would even be funny if they didn't lead to such blazing conflicts. Parents end up saying, "I just want my kids to love each other! I want them to love each other the way I love them."

Isn't that how God must feel when He sees His children fighting with each other? When God sees Christians at odds with each other, fighting and arguing over nonsense, He must say, "I wish just one of them would lay down his rights and say, 'You know, this is not all that important. What's really important is for us to love each other.'"

Those are, after all, Jesus' marching orders for His followers. As He was getting ready to shove the disciples into the world, Jesus basically said, "Listen! You're on your own now, but I'll send the Holy Spirit to help you." (That's my loose paraphrase of John 14.) He went on, "Here's the bottom line: L-O-V-E. I want you to love each other. I want you to put the other person first. If people get one impression from you, it ought to be a strong impression that you love each other!" (Read Jesus' full color commentary in John 13 and 15.)

If you're really serious about making choices that please the Lord, you will need to come to grips with the relational considerations and practice a boat check as you make decisions. The questions you will need to regularly ask yourself are the following:

1. Would I want this done to me?
2. Will this decision appear wrong to someone, even though it's right?
3. Will this choice cause a brother or sister in Christ to struggle spiritually?

And underlying all of these considerations is love.

The Gut Check

This is, of course, the check we've been waiting for. It's the one we practice instinctively: *How will this choice affect me?* Instead of approaching it first, however, we should always approach this step with the God check and boat check in mind. Our personal considerations never trump spiritual and relationship considerations. And the three gut check questions may not be quite what you're expecting.

The decisions in question still fit in the general category of decisions we need to make. We want to live within the parameters of God's Word, and we want to make choices that please Him. In the area of internal considerations, I can ask three clarifying gut check questions. These form the final grid that helps inform decisions that meet the standards of wisdom.

The first gut check question is this: ***Will this choice bring me under the power of something?***

Say what? In the words of 1 Corinthians 6:12, **"'All things are lawful for me,' but not all things are helpful. 'All things are lawful for me,' but I will not be dominated by anything."** Even if something is allowed, is it helpful? Even if something is permissible, could it morph into something that controls you?

Let's put this in a live context. On the questionable list are some areas open to interpretation, such as

- Music
- Alcohol
- Chocolate (I'm kidding!)
- Movies
- Smoking
- Recreational drug use
- Inappropriate settings
- Certain forms of debt
- Other (I'm sure many Christians could fill in the blanks.)

Are these areas in which we're experiencing freedom or slavery? Paul writes, **"I will not be mastered by anything"** (1 Cor. 6:12 csb). As Christians, we are expected to function under the power of the Holy Spirit. We have only one Master, the Lord Jesus Christ. We want to do what God wants us to do. As a result, we want to avoid things that are potentially addictive for us, that draw us into bondage, or that enslave us.

What about alcohol? On a hot button issue like alcohol, the primary biblical teaching starts with, "I will not be brought under the control of anything." You and I have to wrestle with what that means. Does that mean moderation? What is moderation? Moderation is not a single standard that can be applied to everyone. I can't tell you what moderation is for you. My alcoholic friends tell me that moderation is a myth, and freedom for them means not a single drop of alcohol. They can only moderate by completely abstaining. Might alcohol enslave you?

Some readers may think drinking in moderation is a fine thing. Based on what I've been explaining in this book, I'm convinced that it's your choice, and you'll account to God for it. Just as those who are addicted to caffeine might wonder whether that's a different form of bondage. Those who never touch a drop of alcohol yet can't function without fifteen cups of coffee by 10:00 a.m. might be experiencing a bondage all their own. Does God care about that? Believe it. God only wants you to be under one power: Him. He doesn't want you to be enslaved by or addicted to anything.

Some people are addicted to a relationship. They think they cannot be happy in life unless their marriage is perfect.

They are enslaved to a certain ideal or expectation that will drive their mate crazy! That's too attached, and it's wrong. God hasn't designed us to meet all of one another's needs—that's His job.

Some people are addicted to their children. They are obsessed with their kids so much that it's unhealthy. Kids may love the attention, but they weren't designed to be the center of the universe. When people think the sun truly rises and sets on their kids, not God, they set themselves up for deep disappointment, and they raise unhealthy kids. And that's wrong.

Slavery can take many forms. If we want to be wise and free, then one of the best decisions we can make is to break all addictions except submission to the lordship of Christ. That's a big deal in wise decision-making. If you make and live out that decision in your life, you will please Him.

> If we want to be wise and free, then one of the best decisions we can make is to break all addictions except submission to the lordship of Christ.

The second gut check question is this: *Can I do this with confidence that it's right?*

In other words, are you sure it's right? Back to Paul and the Corinthians' meat-eating dilemma. **"The faith that you have, keep between yourself and God. Blessed is the one who has no reason to pass judgment on himself for what he approves.**

But whoever has doubts is condemned if he eats, because the eating is not from faith. For whatever does not proceed from faith is sin" (Rom. 14:22–23).

Happy are those who makes choices they know in their hearts are right! Paul was addressing meat, but the subject of appetites applies to many aspects of life. **"But whoever has doubts is condemned if he eats"** reminds us not to treat our personal convictions lightly.

Let's say I'm at Mike's house, and he invites me to stay for dinner. If he sets out a huge platter of vegetables and a juicy pot roast made from meat I know was offered to idols, I have a decision to make. Perhaps I'm not sure if this is really right. Meanwhile, Mike's more mature than I am, and he already knows it's fine. He shops the meat market without hesitation because he agrees with what Paul wrote, **"I know and am persuaded in the Lord Jesus that nothing is unclean in itself, but it is unclean for anyone who thinks it unclean"** (Rom. 14:14). He doesn't think it's unclean, so it's fine. But if I'm uptight about whether it's right or not, then it would be wrong for me to eat. It's wrong to do something, even if it isn't wrong, if you're not confident it's right. And if Mike is mature, then it's his duty to graciously accept my hesitation, recognizing that my conviction is acceptable even though it differs from his.

This is the point of a gut check—giving your convictions a chance to speak. If you are standing outside the movie theater, saying to yourself, "I don't know if I should go to this movie. It has mixed reviews, some questionable content . . . oh, let's just go see it." That's a wrong choice, even if it isn't wrong. It's wrong to do something unless you're confident that it's right! **"For whatever does not proceed from faith is sin"** (Rom. 14:23). If I can't choose something with confidence that it's right for me to do, then I shouldn't do it. If in doubt, don't.

The third and final gut check question is this: *Am I breaking any previous commitments?*

We live in a day and age where people's word is not their bond. Too often, a person's "commitment" is more like the thermometer of how he feels at the moment. When the winds change, he'll do as he pleases, regardless of what he told you he'd do. In other words, we live in a time where genuine integrity is a rare find.

Our promises need to be simple, direct, and dependable. Jesus said, **"But let your 'Yes' be 'Yes,' and your 'No,' 'No.' For whatever is more than these is from the evil one"** (Matt. 5:37 NKJV). Jesus' half-brother James echoed his brother's words. **"But above all, my brothers, do not swear, either by heaven or by earth or by any other oath, but let your 'yes' be yes and your 'no' be no, so that you may not fall under condemnation"** (James 5:12).

A special appreciation for integrity can be found throughout the Old Testament. Psalm 15 describes the one who dwells with God, someone **"who swears to his own hurt and does**

not change" (15:4). God commends people willing to suffer rather than break their word. He is pleased by those who are willing to keep their word, even when it costs them dearly. Solomon reminds us, **"When you vow a vow to God, do not delay paying it, for he has no pleasure in fools. Pay what you vow"** (Eccl. 5:4). God hears our promises, whether they're directed to Him or to other people, and He expects us to keep our word.

If you don't think this is a huge problem among God's people today, think again. It's sad when people want to hide behind the excuse, "Well, this is God's will for me." God's Word clearly teaches that it's never His will for you to break your commitments. And that doesn't refer just to commitments to God. When we walk to the front of the church, take someone's hand, stand before God, and vow, "Till death do us part," that's a commitment. God hears those words! And if you have any choice in the matter (I realize that when two people are involved, sometimes the choice isn't yours alone.), and you want God to be pleased, keep your commitments. When you get a job and tell your boss, "I'll work this many hours/months/years," keep your commitment. Do what you said you'd do! That's God's will—even when it costs you. If you want to know what God's will is, then here's a good starting point: keep your commitments. God's really into that. And He certainly keeps His commitments; otherwise, you and I wouldn't stand a chance!

If we want to be like Jesus, let's keep our promises. If we say we will do something, then let's do it. Let's choose our words more carefully. Let's not make promises we can't or won't keep. It's better to say "no" than to say "yes" and let others down. Let's keep our commitments. God is pleased by that.

In Luke 9:57–62, Jesus makes some remarkable statements about discipleship. People were approaching Him with unwise or conditional promises of obedience. Jesus' last words to the group that day were, **"No one who puts his hand to the plow and looks back is fit for the kingdom of God"** (Luke 9:62). Jesus wasn't talking about farming but about living. And He wasn't describing plowing but decision-making. We demonstrate our fitness for the kingdom of God by the way we make decisions and keep our promises. He gives us the freedom to make choices and is pleased when we keep the commitments we make.

> The God check preserves vertical freedom; the boat check and gut check preserve our horizontal freedom.

God gives us real choices to make, and through His Word He has given us the necessary wisdom to choose well. We can please Him. In our decision-making, we can honor Him first by doing a God check on our choices. We can love our neighbors by doing a boat check. And we can be true to ourselves by doing an honest gut check before we decide. The God check preserves vertical freedom; the boat check and gut check preserve our horizontal freedom.

And Christ is honored.

Lord God,

Thank You for the freedom You've given me. It's scary, in a way; part of me wishes You had simply laid out a blueprint for my life. Making all these choices in life is a big responsibility. But because of the freedom You've given me, I can, in a meaningful way, please You. Thank You for that opportunity, Father, and help me to make wise choices that please You. Help me to develop the disciplines of thinking carefully through my choices in light of pleasing You, loving others, and honoring my own convictions and commitments. Teach me to keep my word, even when it hurts. Teach me to love others as I want to be loved. Open my eyes to see that being loving is always more important than being "right." In Jesus' strong name I pray. Amen.

CONCLUSION

WE'VE COVERED A lot of ground. You survived eight, intense chapters and perhaps some seismic shifts in your thinking. Congratulations, and welcome to the freedom of living in God's will! Along the way we debunked the widespread but flawed idea that God has a detailed, specific, individual blueprint for each of His children's lives. We discovered that God's will isn't about the silly minutiae of life (which car/couch/cat/college/etc.) but about *who we are*. God is all about our sanctification: that refining process in which we are conformed more and more into the image of Christ Jesus. We affirmed that God's sovereign will is the combination of God's secret purposes, plan, and power that controls the outcome of all matters in the universe, and nothing thwarts God's sovereign plan. While God's sovereign will is His business, He has made His Word our business. This is why we say, "The will of God *IS* the Word of God." The Bible includes all the specifics God commands us to obey as our means to participate personally in accomplishing His sovereign will. We discovered the wonderfully emancipating notion that God's will for His children *IS*, quite simply, His Word. Within the broad boundaries of God's Word, we find incredible freedom.

With these liberating truths in mind, may I offer some final suggestions?

1. Believe and live every moment the reality of God's abiding love for you. It took me many years to shake the destructive backdrop of God's furrowed brow and frowning face. In the words of the humorist Jack Handey, famous for his Deep Thoughts, "If a kid asks where rain comes from, I think a cute thing to tell him is 'God is crying.' And if he asks why God is crying, tell him 'it's because of something you did.'"[6] Is that how God relates to us? No! If you have embraced Jesus Christ as your Savior by faith, then God is delighting in you today as His son or daughter. He is rejoicing over you with singing (Zeph. 3:17). He has called you by name, and you are His own (Isa. 43:1).

2. Let's be gracious with those stuck in the old, unbiblical paradigm. When you get the "it's God's will" verdict dropped on you in an effort to suppress biblical things like praying for wisdom, searching the Scriptures, and personal accountability, don't react with pride or superiority, but with grace, patience, and gentle persuasion.

3. Let's purpose afresh to spend more time in God's Word, feeding on and familiarizing ourselves with His written Word. How else will we truly know His will? We now know, more certain than ever, that the will of God *IS* the Word of God.

4. Let's make our focus true Christ-following, in which the character of our conduct and the tone of our conversation are actual, conscious efforts to imitate the Christ of the Gospels and all of God's Word. Let's harbor no rationalization of personal behavior that doesn't conform to the very steps of Christ (1 Pet. 2:21).

5. Let's see the difficult things we face not as evidence that God has abandoned us but instead as the Shepherd rolling up His sleeves and moving to exert His will in making us more like Himself—for that in fact *IS* His will.

My heart for you in every page of this book is that you would step more fully and more consistently into the glorious liberty of the children of God, sense His great pleasure in you today, and say continuously as you never have before, **"I delight to do your will, O my God"** (Ps. 40:8).

ACKNOWLEDGMENTS

EVERYTHING, AND I mean EVERYTHING, pales when compared with the surpassing priority of doing the will of God. But there has been so much confusion and sadly manipulation that it has become nearly impossible to have a rational discussion about what the "will of God" actually *IS*. Thank you, readers, for joining that conversation and opening your minds and hearts to the truths of God's Word. I am so thrilled that you picked up this book, and I believe with all my heart it can revolutionize and bring immense clarity to the primary lens through which you view all of life. **"I delight to do your will, O my God"** (Ps. 40:8) is where we want to live, but of course to get there, we have to dispense with all the private mysticism and public assertion contrary to what the will of God *IS*. I trust that through the journey of these pages, we got there together.

As we conclude, I have to do God's will myself. Paul told the Thessalonian Christians that among other things, giving thanks in everything was an essential ingredient in what the will of God *IS* (1 Thess. 5:18). I want to thank our faithful friends at LifeWay who have been long-time partners in curriculum publishing, but only two other times have we published a book together. We offer this volume to you in hopes of doing more together, and I am grateful for your commitment to my ministry and faithful friendship through the years, especially Thom Rainer, Bill Craig, Eric Geiger, and more recently, Jennifer Lyell and Devin Maddox.

A special thank you to Garry Friesen, whose book *Decision Making and the Will of God* opened my eyes to the fallacy of the dot and introduced me to the biblical freedom of God's will. I highly recommend this book for further reading on the subject. Another treasured book on the will of God is *Decision Making by the Book: How to Choose Wisely in an Age of Options* by Haddon Robinson. For further reading, also see John MacArthur's practical little book, *Found: God's Will.*

I am also grateful to the Lord for our team here at home. Janine Nelson has been the Executive Director of Walk in the Word for well beyond a decade, and the message God has given me would not be around the world daily without her exceptional leadership and devotion to serving Christ with us. The original messages were faithfully transcribed by our ministry partner of more than twenty years, Rosa Sabatino.

Paige Drygas, always cheerful and exceedingly capable, has been my in-house editor and devotional partner for several years, and the miles since her move to Atlanta have not diminished our joy nor my thankfulness to be serving the Lord together through these written words. Sharon Kostal and Jenn Hawkins administrate my time and are deeply appreciated for keeping all things on schedule and in the right order. My wife, Kathy, always yielding time that could be hers so we can feed God's people through God's Word, is truly the best woman I know and the source of God's constant grace in my life. For thirty-three years she has done the will of God as a loving wife and mother to our family, without whom I would be unknown to you and unused by our Lord. Our family is always the backdrop to any ministry I am blessed to bring your way, and their service to Christ by our side, along with five grandchildren now lighting our lives and watching our example, are sufficient motivation to keep God's will as our highest priority and focus. Thank You, Lord; Your will *IS* my sanctification. The preaching and writing of these truths have sealed that reality to my heart, and I am deeply grateful to be a **"vessel . . . of clay . . . marred in the hands of the potter . . . that He remade . . . as it seemed best to the potter to do"** (Jer. 18:4, author's translation).

NOTES

1. Garry Friesen, *Decision Making and the Will of God* (New York: Multnomah Books, 2004).

2. Describing God's will as a "dot" draws from Garry Friesen's profound book *Decision Making and the Will of God*, a rich, in-depth exploration of the topic of God's will for those who want further study.

3. Garry Friesen, *Decision Making and the Will of God* (New York: Multnomah Books, 2004), 115.

4. John MacArthur, *Found: God's Will* (Colorado Springs: David C. Cook, 2012), 74.

5. Haddon W. Robinson, *Decision Making by the Book* (Grand Rapids: Discovery House, 1998), chapter 2.

6. See http://thinkexist.com/quotation/if_a_kid_asks_where_rain _comes_from-i_think_a/338729.html.

FOR DEEPER STUDY

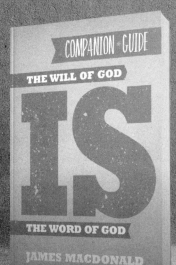

The Will of God Is the Word of God Companion Guide will help you go deeper with the truth about God's will. These searching questions and discussion guides will help you and your community wrestle with God's will for your life.